CHILDREN OF THE 12 TRIBES

BERNIE GOLDING

First published by Diversity Network Australia 2020
Copyright © 2020 Bernie Goulding

ISBN

Paperback - 978-1-922372-42-0
Ebook - 978-1-922372-43-7

Cover design: Ultimate World Publishing
Layout and typesetting: Ultimate World Publishing
Editor: Hayley Ward

DIVERSITY NETWORK
AUSTRALIA

Diversity Network Australia
North Melbourne
Victoria Australia 3051
www.diversitynework.com.au

TESTIMONIALS

I have thoroughly enjoyed your book, Colour *Outside The Lines: One Girl, Two Tribes*. The storyline is captivating as both Fijians and Australians alike can relate to your experience. The appeal and relevance of the book to all bi-racial readers is very clear from each page and chapter. Your book adds to the increasing number and proud collection of stimulating historical and anecdotal accounts by Fijian authors about the rich tapestry of Fiji, the Pacific and her people throughout our evolution over the years. It is a very well written exposé of 'One girl, two tribes.' May more Fijian writers follow!

**His Excellency Luke Daunivalu,
Fiji High Commissioner to Australia**

Working under Bernie was a huge learning curve. She taught me to embrace my ethnicity and cultural background and use it to positively set myself apart from the crowd. Previously I had viewed my diversity as a hindrance to career success and had struggled to get ahead in corporate settings. It was comforting yet encouraging having a successful, strong female from a minority group in a position of influence. This gave me the courage to push even further in my career. One thing I truly appreciate about Bernie is that she was passionate about my growth and yearned for me to succeed more than I wanted it for myself. I am now very comfortable to be a young female from a minority background who is in a position of influence, not just to tick the diversity box, but because I am smart and exceptional in what I do.

Lorraine Makumbe – National Injury Manager

Knowing Bernie as a colleague, a mentor and, above all, a friend has given me a small but impressive insight into how she thrives as a Fijian Australian. In the corporate world, from boardroom to factory floor, as a professional, in the playground as a mother, and around the family dinner table as a wife, sister, daughter, aunt, cousin and niece, Bernie is giving of her expertise, technical knowledge and life experience. You are always in good hands with Bernie as her selfless approach ensures you walk away better for seeing her – always having had a good laugh along the way. She gives from the heart with the smarts of the mind and her story of life is more than just a life story – it wonderfully intertwines with yours through the various roles she plays in the multiple contexts in which she lives.

Cathy Vickers – National HR Manager

Thank you for penning such a wonderful book. I read it effortlessly and really enjoyed it. There are so many things I want to now discuss with others. I have purchased a copy of your book to donate to our school library and hope to spread your amazing message to our beautiful multicultural young ladies at our college.

Penny Curtis, Killester College

Bernie has been one of the biggest influences and mentors in my life and career. She has enabled me, coached me and given me the confidence to move beyond my comfort zone and continue to explore my true purpose. She is honest, highly professional and has strong moral principles. Bernie's Australian and Fijian qualifications and connections translate into her innate ability to fully appreciate sociocultural issues from multiple perspectives. These cultural and social aspects of life can both connect and separate us, yet she is able to create an atmosphere of acceptance that radiates through interactions with others.

Workplaces can be chaotic, yet Bernie has an amazing sense of calm about her and adopts a logical approach, which has had a huge impact in showing me how I want to move through the world. Plus, she is able to bring a sense of fun to what can be tough working environments. Being able to work with people of different backgrounds, at different levels and in different settings is not an easy thing to achieve, yet this is one of her biggest skills and it is clear she can lead the way to a more connected and compassionate world.

Celia Prosser – Regional Manager,
Health, Safety & Wellbeing

Bernie entered my life when I was most vulnerable. I thought I would never recover and that my life was not worth living. She showed me a path towards happiness. Her advice to me reflected on her diversity, not only cultural but also spiritual. She is so open-minded and accepting of me and helped me to realise that although I have experienced some very dark times, life is an adventure worth living. I would like to thank Bernie for reminding me what it was like to have a laugh and being such a good friend and mentor to me.

(Name withheld)

Bernie led the formation of the Fiji Royal Life Saving Society because the drowning rate was so high compared to other countries in the Commonwealth. To increase water safety awareness and lifesaving training throughout the Oceania region, Bernie partnered with the University of the South Pacific and introduced the lifesaving instructor course, supported by the University Faculty of Education and the Royal Life Saving Society of Australia. Students from the twelve member countries were given the opportunity to participate, including the Cool Islands, Kiribati, Marshall Islands, Nauru, Niue, Solomon Islands, Tokelau, Tonga, Tuvalu, Vanuatu and Samoa. Hundreds of local children also attended water safety and swimming with great success.

Albert Miller
Fiji Olympian and Coach,
ex University of the South Pacific

A wise man once told me, we (Pacific Islanders) are not separated by land, we are all connected by water. It's all one tribe, all one nation. We are the seafaring people.

Jason Mamoa

Aquaman

Our Oceania Tribes, Artist Mikaela Goulding

DEDICATION

This book is dedicated to the *Children of the 12 Tribes,* of all abilities, including:

Australian Aboriginal and Torres Strait Islander Communities
Cook Islands
Fiji
Niue
Papua New Guinea
Timor-Leste
Tokelau
Tonga
Samoa
West Papua
Vanuatu
New Pasifika Communities

Writing this book with the children of the Pacific has confirmed what I always suspected was true; we are all connected, and our ancestors were all one people.

Vinaka vaka levu and thank you for sharing your traditional stories. My hope and prayer for you is that you are allowed to develop your

Indigenous five senses of security, belonging, identity, purpose and wellbeing. These are your superpowers which can give you strength, knowledge and resilience. I believe that with them, you can help make our world better for future generations of our 12 tribes.

Vinaka vaka levu and thanks to you, the person interested enough to buy our book and listen to our stories. All sale proceeds from *Children of the 12 Tribes*, will be distributed amongst the participating communities, with priority given to those worst affected by the COVID-19 pandemic and Tropical Cyclone Harold.

Loloma and love,
Bernie Goulding

Note From The Author

All the stories, translations, advice and concepts within this publication are written by Pacific Indigenous children, young people and elders across the region and are for general comment and not intended as specific individual advice. Whilst attempts have been made to verify information provided in this publication, neither the authors or publisher assumes any responsibility for errors, omissions or interpretations here. Should readers choose to make use of the information contained herein, that is their decision. It is recommended that readers obtain their own independent medical, financial and cultural advice prior to implementing any recommendations contained within this book.

CONTENTS

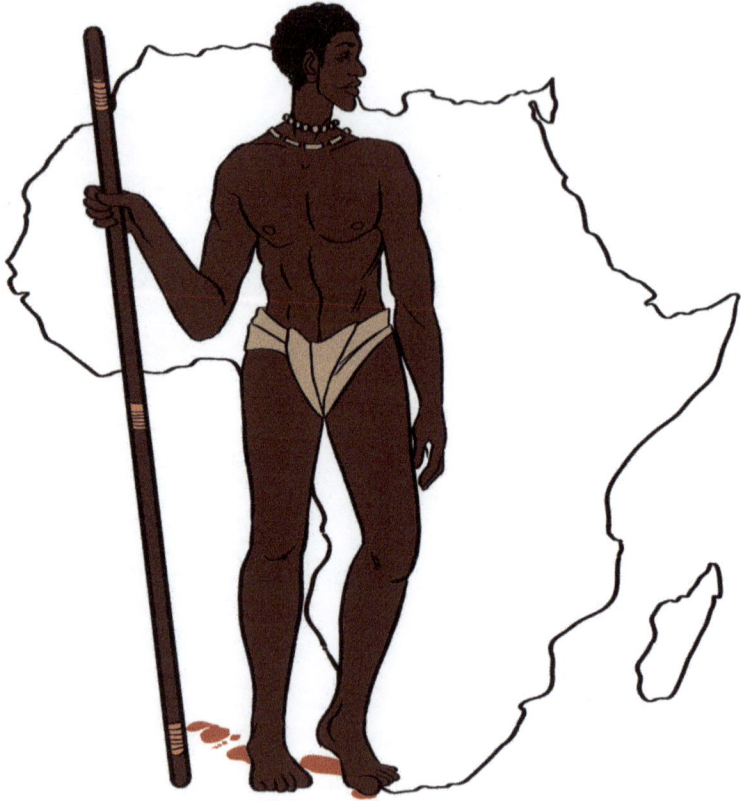

We might have our differences, but we are one people with a common destiny, in our rich variety of culture, race and traditions.

Nelson Mandela

iNTRODUCTiON

More than 60,000 years before Noah built his ark, Aboriginal and Torres Strait Islander people had already settled in Australia. Forty-five thousand years before Abraham was born, Papua New Guinean and West Papuan people were establishing villages and communities on their island of New Guinea. More than 30,000 years before Joseph was given his coat of many colours, people in Timor-Leste were creating art in their caves for their descendants to find.

Later, as Moses was leading the Israelites out of Egypt, ancient Pasifika voyagers were crossing vast oceans and set their sights on Fiji and Vanuatu. When Jesus was born in Bethlehem, Tongan and Samoan villages had already been established for 1000 years. During the Middle Ages, when the crusades were being waged in the Middle East, double-hulled canoes called druas, kalias and 'alias carrying up to 200 people, sailed expertly throughout the Pacific Ocean, to the Cook Islands, Niue and Tokelau, taking food, new knowledge and traditional skills along with them.

The history of our 12 Indigenous tribes is rich and long. Our ancestors' spiritual gifts, connection to the natural world and their astounding knowledge of the ocean and community approach to life, are still poorly understood by the modern world. European colonisation, war, disease and climate change have damaged but not destroyed the 12 tribes. Finally, the rest of the world is waking up and realising there is knowledge and natural riches, worth more than the money they make from drilling for oil and digging for gold and is critical to all our survival. Finally, they are starting to pay attention.

The United Nations (UN) was founded in 1945 after the Second World War and now has 193 Member States or countries. The UN Secretary-General is the leader of the UN and a spokesman for the interests of the world's peoples. Representatives from each of the Member States make up the General Assembly, and they work together on global issues such as peace, security, international law and climate change.

In 2007, the UN General Assembly voted to adopt the United Nations Declaration on the Rights of Indigenous Peoples (UNDRIP for short). Four countries including Australia, Canada, New Zealand and the United States of America voted against the Declaration for their Indigenous Peoples. They all later changed their vote, acknowledging that governments need to work with Indigenous peoples to ensure the minimum standards necessary for our survival, dignity and well-being, are achieved.

The main themes of UNDRIP are:
1. The right to self-determination
2. The right to be recognised as distinct peoples
3. The right to free, prior and informed consent
4. The right to be free of discrimination.

The culture and languages of Indigenous peoples contribute to the world's diversity and may unlock the secrets to protecting our environment, increasing food security, improving health and wellbeing for everyone.

In 1989, the UN General Assembly voted to adopt the UN Convention on the Rights of the Child (UNCRC), which gives all children, 'no matter who they are, where they live, what language they speak, what their religion is, what they think, what they look like, if they are a boy or girl, if they have a disability, if they are rich or poor, and no matter who their parents or families are or what their parents or families believe or do. No child should be treated unfairly for any reason (UNCRC).'

Key articles from UNDRIP and the UNCRC are scattered throughout Children Of The 12 Tribes, to help you learn about the rights of all children and all Indigenous people.

We have collected simple words, phrases and songs in Indigenous languages, and added them to the short stories, poems and artwork of our Pacific Indigenous children, young people and elders to share their stories, connect our tribes and encourage others to do the same.

There is also a simple DNA Action Plan and checklist, which can be used to ease some of the identity and cultural confusion young people may encounter, and build their senses of security, belonging, identity, purpose and wellbeing, and even embrace the very real superpower of cultural fluidity, walking between worlds.

Vinaka vaka levu, and we hope you enjoy *Children Of The 12 Tribes*.

Bernie Goulding

Every Indigenous person is born with the right to life, to live freely and to be safe and secure. Indigenous peoples as a group have the right to live freely, be safe and secure, and not exposed to violence. Children of an Indigenous group may not be taken away from their family by force.

(Article 7, UNDRIP)

ABORIGINAL AND TORRES STRAIT ISLANDER TRIBE

We are all connected.

All human beings belong to one species called Homo sapiens. This means there is only one race of people on Earth, called the human race. Scientists say that we are all descendants of the same African tribe and that 200,000 years ago, our ancestors left Africa in search of food, water, shelter, safety and a better life.

Along their journey, over more than 100,000 years, the bodies of our ancestors changed, as they adapted to their new environments. Those who settled in cooler climates with less sun became pale-skinned. Our ancestors, who continued through Asia to the warm tropical climates of the Pacific, with lots of sunshine, became darker-skinned. They had more of the pigment called melanin, to protect their skin from the sun's ultraviolet rays. Other changes included the size and shapes of their bodies, the colour and texture of their hair and even the shape of their eyes. Surprisingly though, even after 8000 generations, no matter where we now live on Earth, all humans have remained genetically 99% the same.

Amongst our 12 tribes, the first to arrive more than 65,000 years ago were the Aboriginal and Torres Strait Islanders, who travelled all over the continent and established 250 nations, each with their own language. Our first tribe is still the oldest living culture on Earth.

These ancestors were gifted hunters who ate what they caught and gatherers of edible plants, fruits and seeds. Those who lived by the water caught and ate fish. Those who lived inland ate other animals, perhaps early kangaroos and birds. They made tools for cutting and digging, and others for hunting weapons, such as spears and boomerangs. Their canoes were made from bark from trees. Clothing, nets, baskets and bags were made from different plants and animal skins.

These ancestors became deep spiritual leaders and healers. Dreamtime expresses Aboriginal spiritual identity and connection to Country, to the land. Dreamtime tells of the beginning of life. Different Aboriginal tribes have different Dreamtime stories to teach their people about important aspects of sustainable ways of living. Dreamtime stories also teach about the importance of sharing with people in the community and caring for those who may be vulnerable. Dreamtime teaches young people about the importance of looking after Country and all of its creatures.

*The story which has been passed down from generations
tells of three migrations that have occurred over many
thousands of years, one of us coming to this ancient land
first, then another at a period after the last Ice Age which
saw the formation of the Great Barrier Reef, the other is of a
migration out of Cairns that went back through the Cape into
the Torres Strait to PNG and further.*

Gudjugudju
Gimuy Yidinji Cairns Rainforest People Elder

*The Convention (of the Rights of the Child) applies to
everyone whatever their race, religion, abilities, whatever
they think or say, whatever type of family they come from.*
(Article 2, UNCRC)

Torres Strait Islander Fact

Aboriginal and Torres Strait Islanders made great contributions to Australia's war efforts in both World War I and World War II. They were not recognised as real people in Australia back then.

The Torres Strait Light Infantry Battalion was a unique Indigenous battalion who defended not just the Torres Strait but also troops based in West Papua. Almost every eligible man volunteered, although their pay and conditions were much less than white volunteers.

Artist Kanisha Storer, 15 years

In proportion to population, no community in Australia contributed more to the WW2 effect than the Melanesian men of the Torres Strait Islands.

Reg Ball, 1996

IYIL 2019 – International Year of Indigenous Languages

The United Nations proclaimed 2019 as the International Year of Indigenous Languages. Language is, 'at the heart of each person's unique identity, cultural history and memory.' Indigenous languages hold complex knowledge and culture and the United Nations now recognise they are, 'strategic resources for good governance, peacebuilding, reconciliation, and sustainable development,' and are a vital and basic human right for Indigenous People.

Sadly, 40% of the world's 6,700 languages are in danger of disappearing; the majority belonging to Indigenous peoples. More than 100 Aboriginal and Torres Strait Islander languages have been lost, and 110 are now critically endangered. To preserve their Indigenous languages, Aboriginal and Torres Strait Islanders are encouraging :

- Teaching language at home and at school
- Writing books and creating dictionaries
- Recording Elders speaking Indigenous languages.

One of the most unique endangered languages is not spoken. The Yolŋu Sign Language (YSL) of North Eastern Arnhem Land incorporates ancient dance, ceremonies, song and relationships with community and Country. It is an inclusive language for people with hearing impairment and also those with perfect hearing. It may be used when talking is taboo (tabu), during mourning, near sacred places and when hunting.

The important thing about language and what it means is that language contains the essence of the ancestors. Every word comes from place, and identifies people and links to land, country, the dreaming; they are all inherent in language, therefore it means the people, the land, everything.
Yolngu Elder Laurie Baymarrwangga
Aboriginal Senior Australian of the Year

Acknowledgement of Country

I would like to acknowledge the Traditional Owners of the Land on which I have lived and raised my children and grandchildren, the Country of the Wurundjeri people of the Kulin Nations. I humbly pay my respects to their Elders past, present and to those now emerging.

Vinaka sara vaka levu.

Thank you for sharing your Country, your culture and your wisdom with us. Not everyone is ready to accept the gifts that you offer. They do not yet understand that we can all only move forward when we acknowledge the past and seek true reconciliation. I believe that when we are all finally ready to listen, the answers to climate change, good health and wellbeing, and a brighter future for everyone, will be found in your Country and your culture.

Fijian Elder, Robert (Ropate) Young, 85 years

Indigenous peoples and individuals have the right to belong to Indigenous communities or nations. They may not be discriminated against because of their belonging to an Indigenous community or nation.

(Article 9, UNDRIP)

KUNPULU (SAWFISH) JUNIOR RANGERS

I had never been to an Aboriginal community before. I was so excited. I was also terrified. What if I make cultural mistakes? What if I offend?

I arrived in Gurindji country in time for the Freedom Day Festival 2018. So much light, so much colour! I hadn't seen that many smiles in years – everyone here was happy!

I was working with the Murnkurrumurnkurru Gurindji Rangers. Together with the Traditional Owners, we provided opportunities for young people to reconnect with Country and their culture. In one of the hottest places in the world, we controlled feral animals and weeds and built fences to protect sacred places and important water sources.

One of my favourite programs was developing the junior ranger program. 'What will we call it?' I asked the Rangers. 'Something important to us, something that will mean something to the kids from our culture,' they replied. And so it was agreed - the *Kunpulu* (Sawfish) Junior Rangers. The Rangers designed a logo and the school made *Kunpulu* Junior Ranger shirts.

The *Kunpulu* Junior Rangers welcomed me with smiles and enthusiasm. In my time with them, they taught me to laugh, and laugh often. They even tried to teach me to take selfies (I still have not mastered this).

The *Kunpulu* Junior Rangers showed me how they are connected to their culture. They listened to stories told by their elders around the campfire. They practised ceremonial dances and listened to songs being sung by their elders, with the accompaniment of clap sticks.

The *Kunpulu* Junior Rangers showed me how they find fish and turtle – bush tucker. They showed me how to track animals in the desert sand. They told me dreaming stories about their ancestors, about their country, about their culture. Everything is connected.

The *Kunpulu* Junior Rangers inspired me in so many ways. When I see happy kids, when I hear concerns about kids losing their culture, I smile on the inside. Yes, some may struggle sometimes in their personal and school life, but in many ways, these kids are ahead of all of us. They know how to be present and how to laugh. They understand and talk often about their culture. They know who they are. They know what Country they are from. They know who their ancestors are. How many of us can say the same?

Jacqui Young
Central Land Council

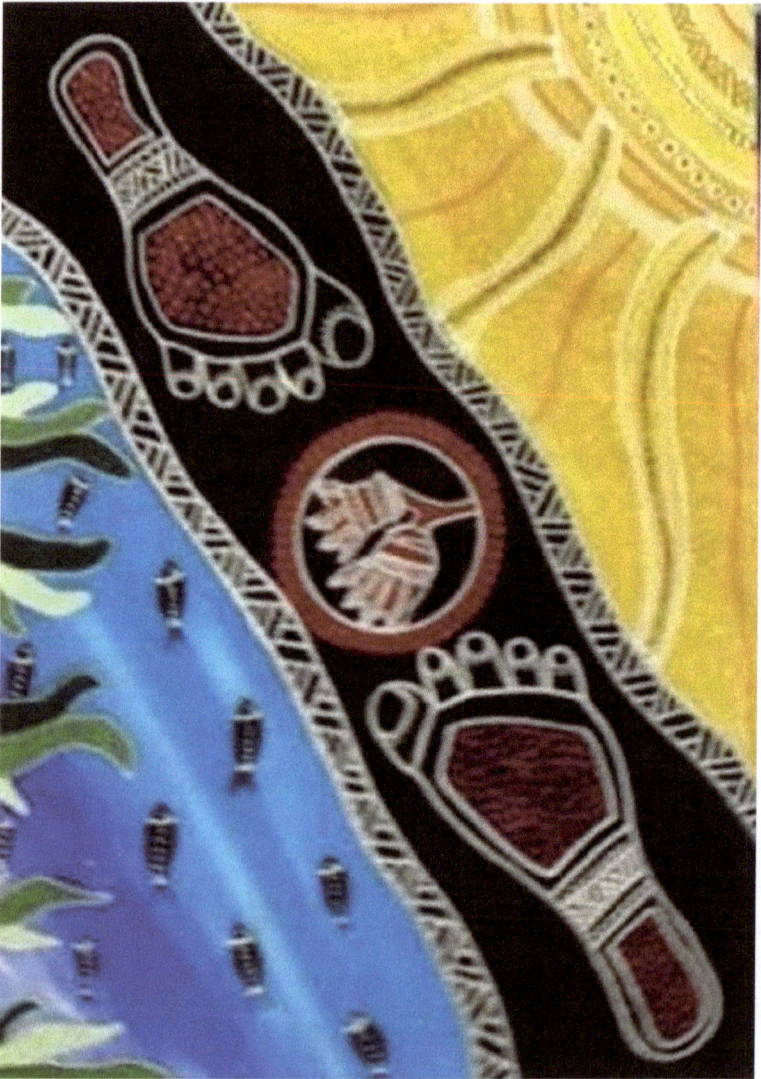

Artist Kanisha Storer, 15 years

Children have the right to live a full life. Governments should ensure that children survive and develop healthily.

(Article 6, UNCRC)

Run Tara Run !

One day, when I was ten years old, I was walking to our local swimming pool, and a girl I knew named Tara, was walking ten metres in front of me. She was really good at sport, especially netball and cross country running. Tara was a year younger than me and was tall, thin, with nice brown skin, bright blue eyes and sort of blonde-brown golden hair. She had a big, bright smile and was always very friendly. I started walking faster, so I could catch up and say hi.

A tram slowed down at the tram stop beside where Tara was walking. Suddenly, people on the tram began yelling, with some waving their fists out of the windows. I froze. There were men, women and children, and they were all shouting. I realised they were angry, and their attention was focused on nine-year-old Tara. 'You brownie, you $@% (swear words)! Go back to where you came from or we'll kill ya!'

I couldn't move, but I looked towards Tara. She was hunched down and looking away from the people on the tram. She didn't seem surprised; she just started walking a bit faster. Then I noticed that some of the people were jostling through the crowd. It looked like they were trying to get off the tram to get Tara. She noticed them too and started to run, quickly turning a corner down a side street and out of sight.

Some of the people on the tram started clapping and yelled, 'yeah, you run! We'll get you next time!' Then, just like that, they settled

25

back into their seats, as the tram started moving again. I turned and walked home instead of going to the pool. I felt sad for Tara and guilty for not running after her to make sure she was okay.

Many years later, I was walking along the same road to pick up my own nine-year-old daughter, Mikaela, from school. 'Mum, I have to fill out a special form, can I tick the Aboriginal and Torres Strait Islander box?' she asked.

I stopped walking, at exactly the same spot I'd stopped so many years ago when Tara was being racially abused. 'We are not Indigenous Australians, your ancestors were from Fiji, Tonga and Ireland,' I replied.

'That's a shame, I thought I was Aboriginal, that would have been cool,' she said and ran ahead to push the button at the traffic lights. I wished I could share Mikaela's profound words with Tara. I hope that wherever she is, Tara is safe and happy and appreciated not abused, for being Aboriginal.

Bernie Goulding

Indigenous peoples have the right to practice and revive their culture and traditions.
(Article 11, UNDRIP)

PAPUA NEW GUINEA TRIBE

We are all connected.

New Guinea was once part of Sahul, the large landmass which includes Australia. Fifty thousand years ago, before the seas rose, our ancestors walked from the Torres Strait to New Guinea. Some may have travelled by canoe. They must have thought that they had arrived in paradise. Nearly a million square kilometres of mountains, tropical rainforest, savanna grasslands, hundreds of islands surrounded by pristine water, containing as much wealth in the sea as there was on the land. Our ancestors must have been very happy here.

European explorers arrived 49,500 years later. Colonisation and wars divided, devastated and re-divided New Guinea. Gold, copper and agricultural riches extracted from the islands, proved to be great incentives for many developed countries. New Guinea was cut in half and claimed at different times by Portugal, Holland, Germany, Japan, Britain, Australia and Indonesia. We now call New Guinea, Papua New Guinea and West Papua.

Papua New Guinea has more than 600 islands and nearly eight million people who mainly identify as Melanesians, though other Pasifika people live there too. Despite their rich sea and land resources, more than 80% of people survive on subsistence farms, and two million people are listed as poor or face financial hardship.

Papua New Guinea people continue to practice their culture, traditions and speaking their 800 Indigenous languages. The importance of equality for women and vulnerable people and the education of children are vital aspects of Papua New Guinea's future.

Indigenous peoples have the right to practice their spiritual and religious traditions.

(Article 12, UNDRIP)

Papua New Guinea Tribe

Theresa

She is a soul – a free spirit with a shell
Caged by duty and bound to love
Her casing contains her flaws and her reflection
But her beauty is contained within the faculties of her mind
For her essence (her grace) are woven by God's design
She had carefully crafted her canvas with linen
Painted over it with tints of blue
And with great caution, her brush glide through
And when her brush ceases to strike,
What will be seen is in black and white.
A thing of focus
Her magnum opus
Her masterpiece is her simplicity
It is born from intricacies yet unknown
And much like the ocean,
She remains more anonymous than the shorelines of the coast
For all shallow waters have been traversed
But hers remain a mystery
Wonderful surface
Dreadful depth
An untold secret
The Ocean's equivalent

Mapusaga Tanuvasa Chou-Lee

A Seed Of Life

A fruit tree produces fruits for today and seeds for tomorrow! In Melanesian society, the past produces the present. In the fruit, the natural power is the physical, social and spiritual power to live, grow and multiply through a holistic process of life.

Thank you Creator for giving and blessing me to this beautiful place called Paradise Of Man In Order. *Klampun yu stap lo lewa blo mi. Yu stap mangal oltaim.* I love you mother land.

Interesting Papua New Guinea Fact

Thousands of Papua New Guinea tribesmen enlisted to assist Australian troops in World War II. They were called the Fuzzy Wuzzy Angels because of their hair, but also because they carried injured soldiers on stretchers over seemingly impossible barriers, finding comfortable places and building shelters to protect the soldiers. Even when under attack, the brave Papua men never abandoned them.

The brave deeds of the Papua New Guinean people, in saving the soldiers, were officially recognised by the Australian Government in 2009, with the presentation of the Fuzzy Wuzzy Angel Commemorative Medallions to those that were still alive.

Artist Isidor Kaupun, PNG

Finding, Owning And Being At Your Best Worth In Life

In a Melanesian society, young ones are encouraged to live in the order of life through:

The Inherited Identities
    i.   Speaking their language
    ii. Knowing their histories
    iii. Singing and dancing in their traditional ways.

Young generations be warned that, 'one's state of being is already lost when one has not found themselves, own themselves and living their best worth above the line. Always live in the spirit of one's identity in life'.

The Integrity of Life
    i.   Respecting the power of feelings and senses
    ii. Managing the power of instincts
    iii. Controlling the power of temperament
    iv. Utilising the power of wise decision making
    v. Acknowledging and appreciating the power of your unique purpose in life.

Young generations be warned that, 'one's dignity and integrity is already destroyed when one has not found their interior self (soul), own their interior self (soul) and living their best interior worth in life. Always live in the spirit of interior order of life'.

The Welfare And Wellbeing Of Life

i. Respecting others

ii. Sharing with others

iii. Motivating and empowering others

iv. Establishing and maintaining ties with others

v. Adding value and complementing and enriching the physical, social and spiritual worth of others.

Young generations be warned that, 'one's welfare and wellbeing are already destroyed when one has not maintained, upheld and strengthened the value of social welfare and wellbeing. Always live in the spirit of common social welfare order in life'.

Isidor Kaupun, PNG

Children have the right to a legally registered name and nationality. Children also have the right to know their parents and, as far as possible, to be cared for by them.

(Article 7, UNCRC)

Indigenous peoples have the right to recover, use and pass on to future generations their histories and languages, oral traditions, writing systems and literature and to use their own names for communities, places and people.

(Article 13, UNDRIP)

Land Security And Sustainable Resource Management For Our Livelihood And Our Future Generations

It is our time, the young generation, to start thinking positively about how we care about ourselves and our future. As changes are happening all around us, it is a must that we have to stop at a point and critically ask ourselves, are we living, sleeping, eating, working, enjoying life and thinking as who we are? What are we doing for our future? Are we going in the right direction? What will the future be like for us and do we still have spare Earth resources in future if life still goes on as it is? Are we prepared for it?

Let us be mindful that the creation that we are living in, gives life and takes life. Remember, we all have land and resources; no man, tribe, culture on Earth lives without land; we were all given enough to share from the Creator. What drives us to have millions of people who are landless, beggars, victims of violence and abuse, shortage of water, oxygen and other resources?

Protect our land. The land provides free services, land, food, fruits, oxygen, water, fish, and animals. The young generation; let us not be blind. It is our time to stand up, protect our integrity, our identity and stand for humanity.

Isidor Kaupun, PNG

Sulka PNG Language Lesson

English	Sulka	English	Sulka
Hello	Veii	One hundred	Mhelom
Goodbye	Mamrung	One thousand	Alo mhel nginta mtiet he hore orom Loktiek
Good morning	Marot	Man	Ngokol
Good evening	Mavlemas	Woman	Vlom
Yes	Eii	Child	Kekayie
No	Nove	Village	Rengmat
Please	Aoo	House	Rek
Excuse me	Tkeis	Market	Mumgu
Thank you	Kanprim	Shop/ Store	A loot to mkor o hirtek
One	Agitgiang	Church	A rek to kam ngarkie
Two	Alomin	School	A mhe to kam lol o papat
Three	Korlotge	Eat	Emik
Four	Korlolo	Drink	Ivie
Five	Aktiek	Sleep	Onit
Six	Aktiek hore orom a gitgiang	Big	Klalout
Seven	Aktiek hore orom alomin	Small	Kasie
Eight	Aktiek hore orom korlotge	Coconut	Ksie
Nine	Aktiek hore orom korlolo	Dance	Ngaerep
Ten	Loktiek	Play	Khanier

10 Phrases

What is your name?	Ila munik ereto?
My name is	Kua munik e
Where are you from?	Ko ngein tam?
I come from	Kotek mo
Where are you going?	Ya ngae ngam?
Where is the ?	Ta vle tam ?
I would like to go to the beach	Kua papat kam ngae ngogu mou
What is this?	A neta?
How much does it cost?	Aner mang?
What is the time?	A ni kolkha ka kek to?

I am against the fact that a settler minority should impose an entire system of values on an Indigenous people.

Steven Biko

South African Activist

SENSE OF SECURITY

Many stories we received from children from our tribes described feeling unsafe and being subject to racist remarks, bullying and physical assault, because of the colour of their skin or their Indigenous background. A 2016 Australian Human Rights Commission survey indicated that 20% of Australians have faced racial discrimination in the form of race hate talk and about 5% of Australians have been physically attacked because of their race. New Zealand's Human Rights Commission also receives, on average, a complaint every day due to racism and discrimination. Another Australian study found that over one-third of students reported racism at school at least once a month, and one-fifth of students experienced at least one form of direct racism every day. The most common experience was being told they 'didn't belong.'

Racist bullying is when someone is teased, mocked, intimidated or shamed because of their physical appearance, ethnic background, religious or cultural practices, the way they talk or because of the clothes they wear. Racist bullying can range from casual but hurtful remarks to deliberate physical and verbal attacks.

Racist bullying hurts the person, their families and communities. The effects can include feelings of sadness and anger, even anxiety and depression. Repeated racism can lead to people withdrawing from work and study and decrease their quality of life. So why is there still so much racist bullying?

Throughout history and colonisation, there has been racism. In 1901, Australia introduced a law called the White Australia Policy, aimed at refusing citizenship and deporting people who weren't white, including Pacific Islanders who had been enslaved to work on sugar plantations.

Assimilation policies were also put in place in the colonies, in the hope that they could 'breed out' the colour and 'whiten' people over generations. New Zealand had an immigration policy strongly influenced by racial ideology, called the Immigration Restriction Amendment Act 1920, which enabled officials to keep Indians and other non-white British subjects from entering New Zealand.

Most racist policies in our region have been overturned, and there are now laws in place that protect people's right to be free from racism and discrimination. However, the old colonial systems are still the foundation of society in our region and ensure white privilege remains in place. White privilege doesn't mean that all white people are rich. It means that you are the racial 'norm' where you live or that white people have more privilege, even if they are not the racial 'norm,' like many expatriates in the Pacific. It means you are:

- widely represented on TV, in movies, social media and in newspapers
- widely represented in picture books, toys, dolls and superhero characters
- not considered part of a minority group where you live
- able to access items which match your skin tone (makeup, clothing)
- likely to be given more education and career opportunities.

White privilege is a system that validates and reaffirms that you are economically, socially and culturally included for no other reason than your skin colour. Other types of privilege include chiefly or class privilege where rank, financial or social status provide benefits or better treatment than those who are not chiefly or considered 'high class.'

What can we do about racist bullying?

Confidence and an action plan can reduce racist bullying and the harm it can cause. Follow the anti-bullying, discrimination and harassment policies at your school or workplace and choose to disengage or disrupt it:

1. Choose to ignore it
2. Choose to say something, if you feel safe, 'Why don't you leave me alone? What you are doing is racist, and it is not okay'
3. Tell a parent, teacher or workplace manager
4. Choose to support those being targeted by staying with them and asking if they are okay
5. Call the police if there is danger.

If you or others are targeted online:

1. Choose to report racist bullying and do not share harmful posts online
2. Report the incident to a parent, the school, your manager or police
3. Choose to make a complaint to your Human Rights / Anti-Discrimination Commission.

Financial Security

Food, water, shelter and warmth are taken for granted by many of us in Australia and New Zealand, but poverty is widespread throughout the Pacific region. Fiji and Vanuatu have the highest minimum wage of our tribes, at just $2.68 Fiji dollars or 14 Vanuatu vatu per hour, equal to just over AUD$100 per week. Timor-Leste had the lowest minimum wage at AUD$44.27 per week. Tonga and West Papua did not have a minimum wage on record.

Food and other groceries often cost more in the islands and remote communities than in the cities of Australia and New Zealand. Housing costs outside of villages are also high. When you add water and electricity bills as well as church contributions, it is easy to see why moneylending has become so profitable in the Pacific and why many people spend their entire working lives in debt.

To combat this, people have become creative so they don't just survive but thrive. Young children help their parents in gardens and sell extra fruits and vegetables in markets or on the side of the road. Mothers often make extra food and set up stalls or walk the streets selling food parcels, cakes and puddings for extra money for the family. Fathers who live near the sea go out with their fishing nets and lines to feed their families and sell their extra fish in the market. Some of the most inspiring people though, are the ones who use their traditional skills to make practical handicrafts and artefacts, like woven mats and baskets, tapa or masi cloth, wooden bowls, clubs and spears and open fired pottery goods such as bowls, water containers, even jewellery. Our ancestors were amongst the first entrepreneurs in the world, bartering goods before money was even invented. If you have a practical skill, why not ask for support and set up your own business?

With a simple finance plan and budget, you can take control of managing your money and avoid moneylenders and credit cards forever. If you have a trusted accountant or financial advisor, seek their assistance. If you don't, you can start with our simple DNA Finance Plan at the back of this book. The plan can help you set goals, pay bills and put aside a regular amount for extended family and community commitments so you are never caught short.

1. 50% – Security expenses including mortgage/rent, food and bills
2. 10% – Extended family, church or community commitment
3. 10% – Pay off loans and credit cards and don't use these anymore
4. 10% – Savings for long term home or business
5. 10% – Savings for children/education

We allocate our income into separate bank accounts each fortnight, using online banking. If you don't have children, the extra 10% goes towards paying off loans and credit cards. When these are paid off, set aside an emergency fund and add to your savings. Every little bit counts.

'Black tax, soli, choking and humbugging,' are terms used in our tribes, which mean the expectation to financially support extended family, church or the village. It is very difficult to say no to extended family and community, especially if there has been a birth, a death, a wedding, sudden illness or job loss. For this reason, many people find themselves having spent all of their next pay before they have even received it. Learning to say, 'I can only give __ dollars' is the hardest part of financial planning amongst our tribes but if you stick to a plan like ours, you can still contribute, stay out of debt and even save money for your own goals, no matter how much or how little you earn.

Keys to a Strong Sense of Security

1. A stable home, food, water, warmth and freedom from fear

2. Racism continues to negatively impact on the health and wellbeing of many people of colour, especially Indigenous people

3. Racism is a learnt behaviour, sometimes triggered by fear of people who are not part of your 'tribe'

4. Having positive role models and a planned response to racism can reduce negative impacts on health and wellbeing

5. A simple budget and financial plan can help ease financial stress and anxiety for individuals, families and communities.

Children should not be separated from their parents unless it is for their own good. For example, if a parent is mistreating or neglecting a child. Children whose parents have separated have the right to stay in contact with both parents, unless this might harm the child.

(Article 9, UNCRC)

WEST PAPUA TRIBE

We are all connected.

When our ancestors arrived in New Guinea 50,000 years ago, there was no line down the middle separating West Papua from Papua New Guinea. Over thousands of years, they journeyed throughout the West Papua side of the island and more than 250 tribes settled there and continued to develop their own languages and cultures. Although they lived in a land rich with gold, oil, copper and natural resources, these hunters and gatherers lived a simple life which remains unchanged for many today. Tribes living high in the mountains hunted with spears and bow and arrows, perhaps eating tree kangaroos and birds, as well as a large variety of rainforest plants. Down on the coastal areas, people continue to hunt and gather plants and enjoy fish and other seafood.

For 49,500 years these ancestors developed their tribal communities and more than 300 languages, making New Guinea the most linguistically diverse place in the world. Colonisation and wars divided, devastated and re-divided New Guinea and it was cut in half, with the Dutch claiming it first and then Indonesia in recent times.

Many people in the Oceania region and around the world support West Papua's ongoing struggle for freedom and independence.

Indigenous peoples and individuals have the right not to be assimilated – meaning, they have the right not to be forced to take up someone else's culture and way of life, and for their culture not to be destroyed.

(Article 8, UNDRIP)

West Papua Child For Freedom

Acknowledgement of West Papua

We would like to acknowledge the Traditional Owners of West Papua and humbly pay our respects to their Elders past, present and to those now emerging. We are grateful for the huge sacrifices made by West Papuan people during World War II when they supported Allied Forces, including Australian and American troops, and saved the lives of many soldiers who were sick and injured during the war. Sadly, many West Papuan lives were lost during the war and afterwards, promises were made for your independence. We acknowledge that your struggle continues today.

We believe that all people, especially Indigenous people, need security, belonging, identity, and purpose, and ultimately this ensures health and wellbeing. We would like to acknowledge your bravery and commitment and we pray for your safety and security, that you have opportunities to strengthen the sense of belonging amongst your people, and that your cultural identity, 50,000 years in the making, endures. May you be supported to remain committed to your purpose and enjoy the sense of wellbeing your people deserve.

Bernie Goulding

Indigenous peoples may not be removed or relocated by force from their lands. If they are relocated, then only with their free, prior and informed consent, meaning that they have the right to make decisions on relocation freely, without pressure, having all the information and before anything happens.
(Article 10, UNDRIP)

Where Else I Should Go?

I grew up in the western part of Papua Island, an island located in the Pacific region, a place inhabited by Melanesians; people who have curly hair and black skin. I grew up in Jayapura city and my home is located next to the beach in Ambora Village. For as long as I can remember, I spent a lot of time on the beach. I felt so peaceful there and enjoyed the natural beauty of life in the village. I saw the beauty of the Pacific Ocean, with the stunning coral reefs, where the fish played and looked for their food. I saw wild pigs in the forest that passed in front of me when I walked into my garden. But when I was seven years old, I had to leave my village and move to the city, because my parent found a new job in Jayapura city. I spent my elementary school and vocational high school years in Jayapura city. After I graduated, I moved to Jakarta to continue my education at the university.

During my education at university, I gained a lot of experience and learnt about economic science, which is my speciality. I studied hard to gain more knowledge about law, and social and political science. From all my discussions, the classes I attended and the books that I read, it all became clear for me. I was able to gain knowledge in Jakarta, but other indigenous Papuans cannot because of poor educational facilities, low literacy levels and no books. These have not been developed for people in West Papua.

Security and being safe is the biggest problem of Indigenous West Papuan people. After it was annexed in 1961, all our natural wealth and resources have been mined and taken. We remain poor, sometimes starving. Although we are separated in the real world from our true brothers and sisters in the Pacific, I often watch YouTube and love to see the 'Haka' performed by the Maoris in New Zealand or listen to 'JahBoy' songs from the Solomon Islands. I feel connected to these tribes, like I am in direct contact with my brothers and sisters, even though it is only via internet.

I often dream of West Papua becoming part of the Pacific someday. I no longer want to be separated from my brothers and sisters. I want to maintain my identity as a Melanesian and live peacefully in my homeland, without global competition for resources that destroys human dignity and the Indigenous culture that I believe in. Indigenous Papuan people cannot wear traditional clothes in court or for important events. Sometimes we are ridiculed or banned. When I was a child, I used to dream about becoming a pilot or a doctor, but I know that there are conditions that make West Papuan people unable to dream about bright futures or even safe ones. I no longer dream of being happy, what I hope is that someday all Papuans are valued as human beings in their homeland; that is my dream right now.

My culture has been destroyed, the dignity of my people has been destroyed, my identity as a Melanesian has been destroyed, my homeland has become a place for illegal miners and for testing new weapons. The blood of my brothers and sisters flows every day. If it is all destroyed and taken, Where Else I Should Go?

Ruland Levy, West Papua

Children of the 12 Tribes

Children have the right to say what they think should happen when adults are making decisions that affect them and to have their opinions taken into account.

(Article 12, UNCRC)

Letters from West Papua

Jow Everyone,

My name is Moses Rumbiak, I am 14 years old and I am from West Papua.

I was born in a village called Saukorem on the Bird's Head of West Papua. It is the best place I could ever imagine because I live between the mountains and the ocean. In my village, everyone is like an auntie and uncle and I have lots and lots of cousins - so many I sometimes even forget all their names. We all associate with one and another every day and everyone knows each other well.

Every morning and afternoon, me and my friends always went to the beach and swim, I really enjoyed that. My favourite part of swimming was when we all went to the deep place of water and it was so much fun. This was natural playground for me and my friends. We really enjoyed it so much. West Papua, our sweet home.

Jow muva,
Moses

Children have the right to think and believe what they want and to practise their religion, as long as they are not stopping other people from enjoying their rights. Parents should guide children on these matters.

(Article 14, UNCRC)

Jow Everyone,

My name is Desty Rumbiak, and I am 17 years old.

I come from West Papua, a small island nation of extraordinary natural beauty. What I like about West Papua is everything. The people, the place, the culture. West Papua is very blessed with natural abundance, with garden fruit and vegetable products and also extraordinary people who have very loving hearts. Togetherness and the kinship of people of Papua is very strong. I am blessed to be born as a West Papua child.

Jow muva,

Desty

Governments should ensure that children are properly cared for and protect them from violence, abuse and neglect by their parents, or anyone else who looks after them.

(Article 19, UNCRC)

West Papua Language Lesson

English	West Papuan / Biak	English	West Papuan / Biak
Hello	Jow	One hundred	Utin user
Goodbye	Jow muva	One thousand	Siar oser
Good morning	Araw bebye	Man	Snon
Good evening	Rob bebye	Woman	Bin
Yes	Imbo	Child	Magun
No	Roba	Village	Mnui
Please	Ibo	House	Rum
Excuse me	Yanbranari	Market	Obe
Thank you	Kasumasa	Shop / Store	Rumbebabo/ Mobebabo
One	Oser	Church	Rumari
Two	Sure	School	Rumfarkor
Three	Kior	Eat	Nanan
Four	Feak	Drink	Aninem
Five	Riam	Sleep	Anenef
Six	Wonen	Big	Beba
Seven	Fik	Small	Kasun
Eight	War	Coconut	Frai
Nine	Fiw	Dance	Fier
Ten	Samfur	Play	Farfnak

10 Phrases

What is your name?	Snom briso?
My name is _____	Snori so _____.
Where are you from?	Ruamuma Kerso?
I come from _____	Yarumuma ker Papua
Where are you going?	Ruaberyo?
Where is the _____?	Diso _____?
I would like to go to the beach	Rayarabe honda
What is this?	Rosarivine?
How much does it cost?	Yabak beso?
What is the time?	Favisu?

Indigenous peoples have the right to set up and manage their own schools and education systems. Indigenous individuals, particularly children, have the same right as everyone else to go to school and cannot be left out because they are Indigenous.

(Article 14, UNDRIP)

West Papua Song	English Translation
Hai tanah ku Papua,	Oh Papua, my land
Kau tanah lahirku	Where I was born and raised
Ku kasih akan dikau	Thee I shall always love
sehingga ajalku	Till' my day of eternal rest comes
Kukasih pasir putih	I love the whiteness of your sands
Dipantaimu senang	On your beaches, joyful
Dimana Lautan biru	Where the azure seas
Berkilat dalam terang	Sparkle bright in the day
Kukasih gunung-gunung	Your high peaks I adore
Besar mulialah	Majestic and grand
Dan awan yang melayang	Sublime clouds, surrounding
Keliling puncaknya	Around the tops, they do
Kukasih dikau tanah	I love this land of mine
Yang dengan buahmu	Naturally abounding with bounty
Membayar kerajinan	That shall pay me off
Dan pekerjaanku	and my labour in full
Kukasih ombak	Thy roaring waves, I am smitten with
Yang pukul pantaimu	
Nyanyian yang selalu	Ever crashing against your white,
Senangkan hatiku	sandy beaches
Kukasih hutan-hutan	A melody that shall eternally
Selimut tanahku	In my heart remain
Kusuka mengembara	I love the sprawling forests
Dibawah naungmu	That this land is built upon
Syukur bagimu, Tuhan,	'Tis rapture to traipse
Kau berikan tanahku	Under its benevolent shade
Beri aku rajin juga	Thank you, oh Lord on high
Sampaikan maksudmu	This land of mine, Thine creation
	Task me to labour ceaselessly too
	To spread Thy cause, far and wide

Indigenous peoples have the right to their cultures and traditions being correctly reflected in education and public information. Governments will work with Indigenous peoples to educate non-indigenous peoples in ways that respect Indigenous peoples' rights and promote a harmonious society.

(Article 15 - UNDRIP)

TIMOR-LESTE TRIBE

We are all connected.

Our ancestor's journey to Timor began more than 35,000 years ago. Like their Pasifika brothers and sisters, they were ancient voyagers and highly skilled at crossing oceans, sailing between islands and catching deep-sea fish with traditional fishing hooks. Some dating back 20,000 years have been found in ancient Timorese caves.

Europeans began to arrive 500 years ago. Colonisation and wars divided, devastated and re-divided Timor. Sandalwood, coffee, oil and later gas proved to be great incentives for other developed countries. So, like New Guinea, Timor was also cut in half and each half claimed at different times by Portugal, Holland, Japan, Australia and Indonesia. We now call Timor, Timor-Leste (East) and West Timor.

Timor-Leste has 15,000 square kilometres of rugged mountains and rainforests, and a tropical climate, with crocodiles, monkeys, snakes, sea turtles, dolphins, whale sharks and 240 different types of birds. Local communities protect Timor-Leste's extremely bio-diverse marine areas, with hundreds of species of fish, coral and sea creatures; many not found anywhere else in the world.

Timorese people are Pasifika as well as South Asian people. Their traditional way of life, religion, culture, community values and even their languages, are linked to Pasifika countries. There is much we can learn from and share with our Timorese brothers and sisters.

Acknowledgement of Timor-Leste

We would like to acknowledge the Traditional Owners of Timor-Leste. We humbly pay our respects to your Elders past, present and to those now emerging. We would like to also acknowledge the huge sacrifices made by Timorese people during World War II when they supported Allied Forces, including Australian and American troops, saving the lives of many soldiers, especially those who were sick and injured. Sadly, many Timorese people were killed or punished for assisting the Allied Forces. Grateful Australians, whose family members were saved, often return to Timor-Leste to acknowledge this sacrifice and pay their respects to surviving family members.

During your struggle for independence, we prayed for you and like thousands of people around the world, we asked our own Government to intervene and support the people of Timor-Leste. Timorese people have taught us that solidarity, sacrifice and commitment to your people can change the world and win, against all odds.

Viva Timor-Leste!

Children who come into a country as refugees should have the same rights as children who are born in that country.
(Article 22, UNCRC)

See My Ability, Don't See My Disability

I dream of a world where people like me, who cannot see, can live a full and independent life where our rights are respected and protected.

I dream that I have learned to use braille to read and write.
I dream that I have learned to participate in life's activities.
I dream of going to school, to work and out in the community, and not being isolated at home.

I dream I have learned to speak, read and write in basic English and Portuguese because I know this can help me find a job and communicate with the world outside of Timor-Leste.

I dream I have learned to use a computer without assistance.
I dream I have learned to play music, to act and create art to express my dreams and aspirations and share my story with the world.

I dream I have friends, co-workers and all the support I need.
My dream can be a reality.

See my ability, don't see my disability.

Gasper Afonso & Luciano Borges
Association of People with Visual Impairment In Timor-Leste
(AHDMTL)

Children who have any kind of disability should receive special care and support so that they can live a full and independent life.

(Article 23, UNCRC)

Balibo

We get up early, our bags packed ready
Five hours on the bus was anything but steady
We pass ladies with baskets, woven tais and orange beads
And eat fish by the sea, in a hut roofed by reeds

We stop at Balibo's pride, the Old Fort Hotel
Bright costumed girls perform traditional welcome as well
We take a deep breath and look all around
Mountains, markets and ocean, then a familiar sound

Shoeless children laugh, chasing a homemade football
Though there's little money, they have fun, one and all
They invite us to join and then run us ragged
We play till it's dark then to the hotel we staggered

We spend a few days in paradise and take time to reflect
From the darkness of war, now stunning at sunset
The people too, more resilient than we'll know
With healed wounds from the past, to a bright future they go.

Bernie Goulding

Pátria

The National Anthem of the República Democrática de Timor-Leste

Fatherland, Fatherland, East Timor our Nation
Glory to the people and to the heroes of our liberation
Fatherland, Fatherland, East Timor our Nation
Glory to the people and to the heroes of our liberation
We vanquish colonialism, we cry
down with imperialism
Free land, free people, no, no, no to exploitation
Let us go forward, united, firm and determined
In the struggle against imperialism
the enemy of people, until final victory
onward to revolution

'How did Timor-Leste achieve freedom and independence against all odds?' I asked, holding my breath and waiting for José Ramos-Horta to reply.

'Solidarity with ordinary people around the world ... Create opportunity and seize it ... Believe in what you believe ... You set your goal and persevere with wisdom ... Use intellect and study, study, study ... Build relationships with humility.'

I scribbled as fast as I could. I think Jose's wisdom may be the answer to many of the world's problems.

Timor-Leste Tetun Language Lesson

English	Tetun	English	Tetun
Hello	Óla	One hundred	Átu ida
Goodbye	Adéus	One thousand	Rihun Ida
Good morning	Dader Díak	Man	Mane
Good evening	Kalan Díak	Woman	Féto
Yes	Los or Sim	Child	Labarik
No	Lae	Village	Vila
Please	Favor	House	Uma
Excuse me	Kolisensa	Market	Bazár / Merkadu
Thank you	Obrigadu	Shop / Store	Loja
One	Ida	Church	Igjera
Two	Rua	School	Eskola
Three	Tólu	Eat	Han
Four	Haat	Drink	Hemu
Five	Lima	Sleep	Toba
Six	Neen	Big	Boot
Seven	Hitu	Small	Ki'ik
Eight	Úalu	Coconut	Nuu
Nine	Sia	Dance	Dansa
Ten	Sanolu	Play	Halimar

10 Phrases

What is your name?	Ita nia naran sa?
My name is _____	Hau nia naran _____
Where are you from?	Ita husi ne'ebe?
I come from _____	Hau mai husi _____
Where are you going?	Ita bo'ot ba ne'ebe?
Where is the _____?	Iha ne'ebe?
(Where is the Baby)	(Bebe iha ne'ebe?)
(Where is the School?)	(Eskola iha ne'ebe?)
I would like to go to the beach	Hau hakarak atu ba tasi
What is this?	Saida mak ida ne'e? or Ida ne'e saida?
How much does it cost?	Ida ne'e folin hira?
What is the time?	Tuku hira?

SENSE OF BELONGING

*For Indigenous peoples, the impact of separating us from
our heritage goes directly to the heart that pumps life
through our peoples. To expect a people to be able to enjoy
their culture without their cultural heritage and their sacred
belongings is equivalent to amputating their legs and digging
up the ground and asking them to run a marathon.*

Mick Dodson
Australian Barrister

We all need to belong. It is a human need. We belong first to our family, our tribe, then the wider community. The relationships we develop as young children are critical to our sense of belonging. Belonging is central to who we are and who we will become. What happens if we don't feel like we belong in the place where we are, and to the people we are with? According to some experts, anger and rage are the results.

'The root of this problem is not fitting into society. We are fiercely social beings and if you are a young individual not fitting into society and failing, you will find a group that will accept you. Many terrorists are fundamentally misfits; they are not successfully integrated and productive in their own lives, so they find a group they can have affinity with. We've seen this for years in gangs, it's the same in terrorism, they want to belong to a group, they have a cause,' says R. Doug Fields, author of Why We Snap.

Anger, rage, disengagement and antisocial behaviour are often linked to not fitting in and a lack of belonging. Media reports often make things worse with their portrayal of people of colour, including our Pacific tribes. According to the Crimes Statistic Agency figures, 2017, Australians are far more likely to be victims of crime committed by other Australian, New Zealand, British or Indian born people, yet media often focus on those of African descent, who make up just 1% of perpetrators of crime, and Pacific Islanders are even less than 1%.

Some governments have put special support initiatives in place, advising, 'Young people in Pacific Islander communities can face a number of challenges, including disengagement from school, experimenting with alcohol and drugs and racism and discrimination,' says Jenny Mikakos, former Minister for Youth Affairs.

'Some of our disengaged young people who have gone off the rails rebel against a society they believe is rejecting them. This is creating a cycle of fear and rejection which, if left unchecked, will continue to grow out of control,' says Andrew Gai, of The Guardian.

Keys to a Strong Sense of Belonging

- Belonging starts with family, then tribe and then community

- A lack of belonging can trigger rage, disengagement and health issues

- Support and acceptance from families, tribes and communities in which we live, is vital and can strengthen our sense of belonging

- If elders are able to share cultural and family traditions, consider recording them to preserve your cultural legacy

- No matter our background, we all have a part to play. Reassurance that uncertainty and struggle is normal and temporary can help increase engagement and develop a strong sense of belonging.

Children of the 12 Tribes

A good government is one with a duty to help everyone, to maximise his or her potential: Indigenous people, people with disabilities, and our forgotten families. We will not leave anyone behind.

Warren Mundine
Australian Aboriginal leader and politician

Children have the right to good quality health care, clean water, nutritious food and a clean environment so that they will stay healthy. Richer countries should help poorer countries achieve this.

(Article 24, UNCRC)

FiJiAN TRiBe

We are all connected.

Our ancestors waited 35,000 years before they journeyed to Fiji. As well as being expert seafarers, they were talented potters, often referred to as Lapita people. The uniquely decorated pottery was used to carry and store food and water and had special cultural and status importance in villages. Although 3500 years have passed, there are still women in Sigatoka and Rewa who make pottery in the traditional ways of our ancestors.

Some say the warrior tribes of Fiji were the most fierce of all. Like their Papuan brothers and sisters, in ancient times, they were cannibals. Some were reported to be seven-foot giants. Dutch and English explorers sailed close to Fiji in search of more treasure and resources, but perhaps chose to keep their distance because of the fierce warriors waiting on the shores.

Fiji would eventually be colonised by the British, but our ancestors were able to retain control of most of their land; they were allowed to speak their own languages and continue to practice their traditional culture and rituals, except for cannibalism of course!

There are more than 300 beautiful tropical islands and oceans full of marine creatures, though no more crocodiles. We think our ancestors ate them all a long time ago. You can still find Fijian people living in traditional grass huts called bures. They still enjoy Pasifika food cooked in the earth oven called a lovo. Tourism and sugar cane have recently been the main industries in Fiji, but many people still live a simple, happy life by the sea, planting a small garden of root crops and leafy green vegetables to feed their family and share with their community.

Indigenous peoples have the right to take part in decision-making in all matters affecting them. This includes the rights of Indigenous peoples to select who represents them and to have Indigenous decision-making processes respected.
(Article 18 - UNDRIP)

Fijian Tribe

Indigenous individuals and peoples have the right to be treated fairly and not be discriminated against in all matters relating to work and employment.

(Article 17, UNDRIP)

Mata Ni Gone

Dad went to see the Governor-General of Fiji and asked him if we could borrow his boat. He was taking our 'faces' to his village, Naroi, on Moala Island in the Lau province, for the first time. This is called 'Mata Ni Gone'. We loaded thousands of dollars' worth of *tabuas* (whale's teeth), farming utensils, reams of clothing material, 20 kerosene drums and non-perishable food items into the boat, to present to our mataqali, our clan.

Hundreds of people were waiting on the Naroi shore to meet us. Dressed in brightly coloured *sulus* and *mumu* dresses, they all looked stunning. Behind them, the remains of Fijian *bures*, blown away or damaged by the cyclone, could be seen. We were warmly greeted then shown to a one-room house with curtain dividers, where my parents and six brothers and sisters would stay. There was an outside toilet some distance from the house and a water tap as well. There was no electricity in the village then, so hurricane lamps were used at night. Woven mats swept clean lined the floor. As we settled in, a group of Fijian women performed traditional singing and *meke* dancing in celebration of our arrival.

'Look how big that knife is!' my brother Peter exclaimed. He was at the window watching two men struggling to hold onto a large goat. One man had a big machete raised over his head. Seven children watched in horror as he chopped off the goat's head. The man was still holding onto its horns, and the goat was still chewing, while its body fell sideways to the ground. Covered in blood, the men dragged the body and the chewing head to the shed near the open fire.

The next day in the same spot, a pig was slit down the middle and villagers began to remove its internal organs. 'It's still alive!' My younger sister Penny said as the colour drained from her face. She was unable to stop staring and decided to become a vegetarian in that instant. The pig, still struggling, managed to jump out of the wooden bowl and ran away, its organs and a long line of villagers trailing behind it. We watched in horror as villagers chased the pig until it finally fell over, dead. The next day chickens were beheaded outside our house of death. The worst though, was the killing of a turtle, which is a delicacy for many Islanders. It is not easy to kill a turtle. The limbs are removed first, then the shell and the head. The turtle cried all the while, and so did the seven children at the window.

Each day there was a special traditional ceremony. My sisters and I were taken by the village women to the beach to go fishing with giant nets. Fully clothed, I was given one end of the long net and my sisters, Lynette and Pauline, were given sections behind me. We were instructed to swim out 50 strokes, turn right, swim another 50 strokes and then turn right again and swim back to shore. All the women then helped to haul in the net full of fish. We had lots of fun, while the women sang and chatted to us in Fijian.

For the most important village ceremony, all of the children were wrapped in traditional tapa cloth and formally introduced to our *mataqali* (clan) leader and the village chief. One of the ladies helping to prepare us told us that being presented to the chief and being accepted by the village means that we are part of Naroi forever. Decades later, I am grateful that my parents followed the traditional cultural ceremonies and observed the Mata Ni Gone in the place of our ancestors.

Bernie Goulding

Indigenous peoples have the right to their own political, economic and social systems, and to follow their own traditional ways of growing food and other activities that help them in their daily living. They have the right to seek justice where this right is taken away.
(Article 20, UNDRIP)

Mana – Lapita Woman

Children have the right to a standard of living that is good enough to meet their physical and mental needs. The government should help families who cannot afford to provide this.

(Article 27, UNCRC)

My Favourite Place

My favourite place to visit is a town called Savusavu
Where everywhere you go, the people always know you
Where everyone's an Aunt and Uncle and the list of cousins
never ends
They call it Hidden Paradise 'cause you're never short of friends

Grandpa George built our family home, it's called Vadravadra
He taught Dad how to plant and share, a gentleman of the
golden era
I never got to meet him but I'm grateful all the same
He worked hard for his family so I'm proud to share his name

There we go to the beach with the big brown boulders
Dad sometimes carries me on his shoulders
We borrow a boat and pile in to catch fish
We share with neighbours, eating from a banana leaf dish

I can't wait to go back and stop in Suva City
The Fiji museum's full of weapons, some are scary, some are
pretty
We can visit Braxton, Baby Kai and Faith, my nephews and niece
Savusavu and Suva, Fiji are where I feel most at peace

Malakai, 11 Years

Fijian Tribe

Children have the right to an education. Discipline in schools should respect children's human dignity. Primary education should be free.

(Article 28, UNCRC)

The Golden Age

I want to tell you there was no Golden Age.

Sometimes people look back and say that things were better before, and opportunities were there for the taking. The reality is that in every generation, life is filled with challenges for us to overcome, to learn from and then move on to bigger challenges. Without challenges, we will never grow.

I am a product of the colonial era.

I was born in Levuka, the old capital of Fiji, in 1935, during the Great Depression. Times were very hard, and my father had to take on all sorts of work to make ends meet. He baked and delivered bread early in the morning, he sewed shirts and trousers for three pennies (cents) and six pennies respectively. I am one of seven children; he had a lot of mouths to feed. Most of my family is Fijian, but my great grandfather on my mother's side was German. My grandparents were from the Eastern Lau Province in Fiji. My father was from Canton in China, so I had no idea to which tribe I really belonged. Sometimes it felt like none.

World War II brought in an influx of soldiers from the United States and New Zealand. It also brought in lots of cash which the locals hadn't seen for some time. Surprisingly, job opportunities became more abundant and people began to breathe easier.

I understand how childhood can be difficult.

My parents separated at the outbreak of the war when the depression was still being felt by all. My mother, Seini Leba remarried and had a baby, but she died not long after. My father did not cope well. We would get a belting if we did anything to annoy him, which was often. In Lautoka we lived in rented rooms and I was often left alone from when I was pre-school age. I recall being called names for wandering around alone, whilst Dad was at work. Somehow we managed to survive till the end of the war.

My father saw an opportunity to open a trading shop in Nabuna, in Koro. We moved there in 1944 with my elder brother, who I met for the first time. The village was a new experience for us and so was the school, which was up in the hills away from the village. The teacher had cerebral palsy and a withered arm and leg on his right side. Students were allowed to lead his horse to and from the school. One morning I decided to do the honours and lead the horse by the bridle. I made sure I was early and went to the teacher's house and sat down and waited. He asked me to collect a book from the bookshelf, which I did. I then lead the horse to the school and felt proud.

At school assembly, the teacher called me to the front and told me to recount the incident regarding his request for the book. I was confused but I relayed my story, to which he replied that I failed to observe the customary ritual of 'Cobo' (clapping of hands as a sign of respect for reaching for the book). In front of the whole assembly, I received a severe caning. I was very hurt and humiliated. I did not know what I had done wrong. I decided then never to return to the school and refused to go back.

I ended up at my Aunt's house at Tamavua, near Suva. Another new experience with 12 children, including my sister Eleni and other cousins under one roof in a tiny three-room house, with a kitchen and a breezeway in between. We were fortunate because my Uncle Morris leased five acres of land with the house. It was hilly and more than half of it was soapstone, but whatever land was available we planted with vegetables to supplement my uncle's income. There were often as many as 20 people to feed but somehow, we worked together and managed. A loaf of bread would have to be shared amongst the whole gang for breakfast. A pound of butter had to last a week; needless to say, we were only allowed to wave the knife over it and could barely taste the butter. Homework was chaos, as we fought over space to open our books. I ended up going to sleep straight after dinner and getting up at midnight to do my homework when the others were asleep.

I enrolled at Marist Brothers Primary School (St Columbus) and later at the Marist Brothers High School, in Flagstaff. As I started late, I had to repeat a year, but then I skipped a couple of classes and ended up with the 'most improved' student of the year award. I graduated with a Cambridge School Certificate; matriculation standard in the old colonial system. I applied for Radiography training at the Central Medical School with an internship at the Colonial War Memorial Hospital.

The Central Medical School, now known as the Fiji School of Medicine, was part of the Nuffield Foundation Grant and attracted students from all over the South-West Pacific area, except for the French Territories. It was exciting to be able to interact with students from other Pacific Islands, sharing and learning about language and culture. I was very fond of an Eastern Samoan student who had polio and had to use crutches all the time, but his disability did not seem to deter him. He later graduated as a Medical Officer.

After working for five years, I applied to further my qualification and experience in Wellington, New Zealand and was successful. Of course, it was difficult to survive there unless you had a bucketload of cash, which I didn't. However, I completed the course and after three years I returned to Suva and requested a salary increase with my new overseas qualification. I was knocked back three times. So I applied for jobs overseas and ended up at St Vincent's Hospital, Australia. During this time, I volunteered to serve as a member of Australia's Surgical Team in Vietnam. Like many Pacific people, I had some initial issues with my visa, but with gentle persuasion I was given permanent residence and now here I am, 50 years, seven wonderful children, and lots of grandchildren later.

So, I am so ever grateful for the cards that life has dealt me with its inherent losses, hurt and challenges. Be mindful, that you will always have the resources you need to stretch you to the next level. Never more, never less. The constant search for fulfilment and happiness can only be addressed with inclusion and support of a community. Be grateful for all the challenges and opportunities that will confront you for they are not the enemies but friends there to support you to the next level.

So my advice to you is, do not buy into the myth of a Golden Age. Have a clear vision and draft your plan to get there. Face your challenges and make your age, the Golden Age. Peace out.

Robert Young, 85 years

Education should develop each child's personality and talents to the full. It should encourage children to respect their parents, their cultures and other cultures.
(Article 29, UNCRC)

Fijian Language Lesson

English	Fijian (Bauan)	English	Fijian (Bauan)
Hello	Bula Vinaka	One hundred	Dua na drau
Goodbye	Moce	One thousand	Dua na udolu
Good morning	Yadra Vinaka	Man	Turaga
Good evening	Bula Vinaka	Woman	Marama
Yes	Io	Child	Gone
No	Sega	Village	Koro
Please	Kerekere	House	Vale
Excuse me	Tulou	Market	Makete
Thank you	Vinaka	Shop / Store	Sitoa
One	Dua	Church	Vale ni lotu
Two	Rua	School	Koro ni vuli
Three	Tolu	Eat	Kana
Four	Va	Drink	Gunu
Five	Lima	Sleep	Moce
Six	Ono	Big	Levu
Seven	Vitu	Small	Lailai
Eight	Walu	Coconut	Niu
Nine	Ciwa	Dance	Danisi
Ten	Tini	Play	Qito

10 Phrases

What is your name?	Na cava na yacamu?
My name is _____	Na yacaqu o _____
Where are you from?	O ni lako mai vei?
I come from _____	O au mai _____
Where are you going?	O lako i vei?
Where is the _____?	I vei a _____?
I would like to go to the beach	Au via lako i matasawa
What is this?	A cava oqo?
How much does it cost?	E vica na kena i sau?
What is the time?	E vica na kaloko?

Bula Maleya (Hello Malaya)

Song written for Fijian soldiers sent to support British troops in Malaya in the 1950s

Fijian	English
Bula Maleya kei Viti talega	Greetings Malaya and Fiji also
Cauravou era yalo qaqa	All the young men are brave
Vosa na wai e vakalasalasa	Talking to the sea gives me
Ni bula ni bula kece sara	happiness
	Hello Hello Everyone
Nanumi Viti vanua lailai	
Nona sasaga me toro cake mai	Remember Fiji, a small nation
Tubu ko Viti me rogo edai	With a will to love forward
Vuravura Maleya me kilai	Fiji will grow to be famous
	For Malaya to be known in the
E da sa mai veikune tale	world
Me noda tu na lagilagi	
E da sa cibicibitaka yani	We have found each other again
Yaca i Viti vua na ranadi	We will celebrate in glory
	We patriotically declare
	The name of Fiji for the honour of
	the Queen

Indigenous peoples have the right to improve their economic and social well-being, and governments will take action to help Indigenous peoples do so, with particular attention to the rights of Indigenous elders, women, youth, children and persons with disabilities.

(Article 21, UNDRIP)

VANUATU TRIBE

We are all connected.

As some of our ancestors journeyed to Fiji, others sailed to Vanuatu. They were also expert seafarers and talented potters, the Lapita people. More than 3000 years ago, together with some of our Papuan ancestors, they settled amongst the 83 islands of Vanuatu. Like many of their Pasifika brothers and sisters, these ancestors were also cannibals, which may have scared away explorers, until France and Britain finally colonised their island home as well, naming the country the New Hebrides. The Europeans came in search of sandalwood, copra and precious metals like gold. Later beef and cocoa would become valued commodities.

Vanuatu recorded the highest disaster risk globally on the World Risk Index last year, due to volcanoes, cyclones, earthquakes, floods and tsunamis. Colonisation and war have not helped either. Yet, the people of Vanuatu have gained independence, maintained control of their land, culture and language, speaking 100 languages, including their national language, Bislama. They continue to live a subsistence farming village life amongst tropical rainforests, beautiful beaches and volcanic mountains and are often voted amongst the happiest people in the world.

It may be a small Pacific Island nation with the highest disaster risk on earth, but Vanuatu is a world leader in the United Nations, bravely supporting Indigenous and human rights; in South Africa against apartheid, campaigning for the freedom and independence of Timor-Leste, and continuing to speak up for West Papua.

At the darkest and most difficult of times, when we were alone and could count on few friends, Vanuatu stood with us. Timor-Leste will never forget this support.

H.E. Xanana Gusmão
East Timorese Politician

Realising Your Purpose

Growing up in a small island nation that contains different lovely communities where there are smiles plastered on almost all the faces seen, is such a blessing. The country itself has twice been voted the happiest place on earth. However, not all things can be said to be 'goody goody'.

Although the natives are caring and supportive towards each other, there are many problems they are facing in each of their lives, and also their society as a whole. These can't be solved due to some factors. Mentioned are some issues that are currently happening: financial issues, natural disasters, poor management of small firms and income, land disputes, health issues, and issues concerning crimes.

These issues keep repeating themselves for the past 40 to 50 years, since Vanuatu has been stepping up in civilisation. A common factor that continues to contribute is, people go to school, but the results are not very effective in the rural communities. Most educated people think there is no employment in the rural areas. As a result, some ended up working in low paid jobs an uneducated person can do for a living, in urban areas, not knowing that there is great wealth in their villages. For that reason, they started blaming the government for not being supportive, when they themselves can't manage and establish small businesses.

As for myself, I grew up in two different societies, in a rural and an urban environment. In these different zones I've learnt about the different situations that people around me are facing. Hence it helps me realise that I have a purpose. In the village where I spent my first years on this earth, I'd seen people lying in their sick beds and not going to the hospital due to the financial constraint. Whereas in the towns there are different kinds of sicknesses that can't be cured by the doctors themselves. Doctors have to work with the support of medical machines, to help the situations their patients are in, to help them become well. When those machines break down, there aren't any medical engineers to fix them. So almost all patients who are supposed to use them wait for them to be fixed or are sent to the capital to be treated.

Getting employed is not for money, status or sustaining yourself, but helping others should be the main goal. Realising the need the people around me are going through makes me think outside the box. 'Medical engineering is what I should be aiming for,' I thought, 'Not for my benefit but for the benefit of others'. Seeing how my community looks up to me by supporting with little things, such as small words of encouragement, food, clothes, other necessary things, helps me see their heart.

Realisation of purpose happens in moments like this, which motivates me to achieve my goal. Through it I can be a help to my family, community and country, in regard to their health issues.

Stacey Kelvin, 16 years

A Good Life

My name is Jay Peter Sumu, I'm 14 years old and I'm from Vanuatu. In this writing, I will mention types of wellbeing examples: physical, spiritual and mental. At the end you will see why it is necessary for a person to master each of these to live a happy and healthy lifestyle.

Physical wellbeing, nowadays non-communicable diseases (NCDs) are very common in Vanuatu. Example, Diabetes. Since we are now living in a civilised society, we often eat sugary and fatty foods and forget our local and traditional foods. We use vehicles as our main source of transportation, rather than walking. So, when consuming these foods and not exercising, we gain extra fat in our bodies which leads to diabetes and obesity. In order to prevent these diseases, we must eat our own local food instead of imported processed foods and do a lot of exercises.

Christianity is something that is being practised throughout the Pacific, yet many people take it for granted. Now that we are advanced in technology, teenagers like me spend more time on social media. Sometimes we spend the whole day inside our homes surfing the internet and playing video games, while we're supposed to spend time with God. Hence the Bible says, 'you cannot serve two masters at the same time, for you will love one and hate the other,' Matthew 6:24. You can't serve both God and your cell phone. In types of situations like this, I suggest we set a particular time aside each day to have personal and quality time with God. God commanded all living things and they came into existence, but he created man with his own hands and breathed oxygen into his nostrils. He created us with a brain. We are very privileged to have this gift, so we must take good care of it. As teenagers, we don't often face stress and depression, but adults face these every day. Stress and depression are caused by worrying due to work, money and other problems in life, which then leads to mental illness. But we teenagers also have mental issues.

You might be wondering how? Good question. I don't know about other countries in the Pacific but in Vanuatu, a lot of young people smoke marijuana and drink alcohol and you can see them roaming around the streets of Port Vila. Research has shown that smoking a lot of marijuana affects your brain. This is proven to us today also, as we have a lot of people here who are facing mental issues due to smoking marijuana. You can prevent stress and depression by socialising with people and doing leisure activities that will keep your mind free of stress. Marijuana use can be prevented by choosing the right peer group and self-control. Our brain is the control tower of our body; we must look after it and use it wisely.

To conclude, we all deserve a happy life, but in order to have one, we must concentrate on our wellbeing and make sure it is balanced. We must live healthy, have faith in God and stay worry-free. This is the end of my essay, I hope you've learned something.

Peter Jay Sumu, 14 years

The Feeling Of Home

Cockadoodle cockadoodle
The natural alarm cries loudly
Cockadoodle cockadoodle
The rhythm was heard
Up above the trees,
lay the feathered alarm
Behind the mountains the old, old bulb was peeping,
readying to show its smiling face
With welcome, the dazzling flowers started the greeting process
From across, lies the mass of moving water that constantly
creates a lullaby song for the villagers
Sea shells are sparkling slightly on the seashore as a result of the
first rays of the sunlight
A little up ahead lies a settlement
The beautiful settlement was like an area of mansions
If you listen closely you can hear the clattering, clambering and
tattering of pots
Definitely it indicates the wake of the whole village. Different
shapes of smoke were forming above kitchen huts
From afar the delicious odour of food can be detected
In each garden of food, soft humming of melodic voices can be
heard from the elders of the village
Shrills of children's laughter sound near the coast
What a feeling of belonging someone can feel
The greeting of neighbours is as greetings of big important
events
You can feel the light tension in the air among the inhabitants

Vanuatu Tribe

Sharing is just instinctive, and respect is the leader
Laughter is like a pop music
Oh, how I wish to go back to where I was before, where the
feeling of belonging is present
How exactly home was
If only time can rewind and then the future generation can see
and feel their true home of belonging

Stacey Kelvin, 16 years

*Children have the right to learn and use the language and
customs of their families, whether or not these are shared by
the majority of the people in the country where they live, as
long as this does not harm others.*
(Article 30, UNCRC)

Vanuatu Language Lesson

English	Bislama	English	Bislama
Hello	Halo	One hundred	Wan handred
Goodbye	tata	One thousand	Wan tausen
Good morning	Gud moning	Man	Man
Good evening	Gud naet	Woman	Woman
Yes	Yes	Child	Pikinini
No	No	Village	Vilij
Please	Plis	House	Haus
Excuse me	Ekskius mi	Market	Maket
Thank you	Tankiu	Shop / Store	Stoa
One	Wan	Church	Jioj
Two	Tu	School	Skul
Three	Tri	Eat	Kakai
Four	Fo	Drink	Drink
Five	Faef	Sleep	Silip
Six	Siks	Big	Bigwan or bigfala
Seven	Seven	Small	Smol
Eight	Eit	Coconut	Kokonas
Nine	Naen	Dance	Danis
Ten	ten	Play	pleplei

10 Phrases

What is your name?   Wanem nem blo yu? _____

My name is _____   Nem blo mi.._____

Where are you from?   Yu blow wea?

I come from _____   Mi blo _____

Where are you going?   Yu go wea?

Where is the _____ ?   Wem _____?

I would like to go to the beach   Mi wantem ko lo solwota

What is this?   _____ wanem ia?

How much does it cost?   _____ hamas lo hem?

What is the time?   Wanem taem?

Governments, with proper consultation with Indigenous peoples, will ensure Indigenous elders, women, youth, children and persons with disabilities have their rights respected. Governments will ensure that Indigenous women and children are free from all forms of violence and discrimination.

(Article 22, UN DRIP)

Sense of Identity

The Indigenous peoples understand that they have to recover their cultural identity, or to live it if they have already recovered it. They also understand that this is not a favour or a concession, but simply their natural right to be recognized as belonging to a culture that is distinct from the Western culture, a culture in which they have to live their own faith.
Samuel Ruiz
Mexican Bishop and Indigenous Rights Campaigner

Your sense of identity is about who you are, the choices you make, what you want to be and what you believe. Your faith and your accomplishments can strengthen your sense of identity. Gender, family changes, a serious injury or illness, and migrating to another country, can challenge your sense of identity.

Many people face an identity crisis when they are forced to tick a box on a form and nominate their race (although there is only one race, humans). People may not look like the cultural background that they identify as, or they have mixed heritage, resulting in them frequently being asked to explain their cultural identity.

DNA ancestry tests have become a popular way to learn about all the different places your ancestors came from. Recent archaeological discoveries in the Pacific have discovered all Pacific Islanders have a mix of Papuan and Asian/Lapita DNA. New Guinea, Fiji and Vanuatu have more Papuan DNA, and Tonga, Samoa and the Cook Islands have more Asian/Lapita DNA. These tests can not only tell how much DNA you have inherited from your ancestors, but also connect you with close and distant relatives. Sometimes the test results are not what you expect, so think carefully before you decide to have one.

Keys To A Strong Sense Of Identity

1. Visit the place of your ancestors and learn about language, history and culture

2. Have positive role models and relationships in your tribe and community

3. Consider a DNA test to trace the path of your ancestors

4. Be proud of your heritage, especially if you have more than one tribe

5. Setting and achieving personal goals can build self esteem and strengthen your sense of identity

People will ask, 'What are you? Where do you come from?' If they do not accept your cultural identity; that is their issue. You can choose to take the good from your cultures, acknowledge the bad or sad history and move forward.

If you can imagine the one family continuously occupying the same land for 40,000 years or more, using it not just to sustain life but as a place of reverence and worship, where every tree, rock and waterhole had significance, you will get some understanding of the importance of land to Indigenous people.

Tania Major
Aboriginal Activist

TONGAN TRIBE

We are all connected.

As some of our ancestors journeyed To Fiji and Vanuatu, others journeyed to the Kingdom of Tonga. The Lapita people settled in the Friendly Isles 3000 years ago and established what would become the only Pacific nation not to be colonised by European powers, maintaining an Indigenous monarchy for 1000 years. The Dutch and the British visited but left Tonga in peace. These ancestors built a society based on *Fefaka'apa'apa'aki* (mutual respect), *Feveitokai'aki* (sharing, cooperating and fulfilment of mutual obligations), *Lototoo* (humility and generosity), and *Tauhi vaha'a* (loyalty and commitment).

Our Tongan ancestors enjoyed living near the beach, with lagoons full of seafood so they never went hungry. Sadly, they ate many of the animals on the islands to extinction, including iguanas and many types of birds. These would later be replaced with domesticated animals.

These ancestors were also expert ocean navigators and sailed throughout their 176 islands and around the Pacific with ease, noting the Tongan empire ruled seas for hundreds of years.

Tonga has been able to maintain their Indigenous language, culture and community values as well as any country in the Pacific and beyond. Technology and modern tourism are now bringing change, however their strong family and community structures have continued the handing down of traditions and stories including the ancient legend of Maui, who pulled the islands of 'Ata and Tongatapu to the surface from the depths of the ocean.

Racist

In primary school, I was bullied because I am Tongan race; other students were coming up to me every recess and lunch and teasing me. They pushed me around. I would come home with cuts and bruises. I cried myself to sleep because I had no idea how to deal with them. I would take a lot of days off to get away from them and I couldn't move schools because all the other schools were too far away. I tried to talk to the teachers, but that didn't change anything.

Students would do more mean things to me and say horrible things about my family and how they would come to my house and beat me up. I didn't want to do anything and some days I didn't even come out of my room. My mother tried to do something, but whenever she talked to the principal, teachers would just talk to those students, yet still they did the horrific things to me. This went on from grade two all the way to grade five.

I finally decided to try harder to make friends with other kids in my class because I thought if I had friends, I could find the confidence to stand up to the bullies. One day, my new friends stood up for me and their friends helped as well. The bullies were too scared to do anything because there was a lot of us that were bigger than them.

Then the next year the principal changed, and I told the new principal what had been happening. So she brought in new rules and made it so if there was bullying, they would have to sit inside her office by themselves and write lines about what they did. This is when finally, the bullying stopped.

Robbie, 13 years

My Positive Role Model

When I received the invitation to write a short story for the Pacific children's writing competition, I was really excited. 'Who is a good role model?' This question was one of choices on the list and it got me thinking. I discussed some famous people at lunchtime with my friends. Michelle Obama, Jacinda Ardern or Lupita Nyongo from the Black Panther. I chose to look back in time and find a Tongan role model instead.

She was born in 1900 and she died in 1965 but many people say she put Tonga on the world stage. Queen Salote was sent to school in New Zealand when she was only 9 years old and she became Queen when her father, the king died. She was just 18 years old and the First World War was ending. She was 6 feet and 3 inches tall and stood tall and proud for Tonga. Queen Salote was an artist, a dancer, a poet and songwriter and a strong female leader a century before Michelle, Jacinda and Lupita. She preserved peace and our Tongan history and traditions.

During the Second World War Queen Salote did fundraising and built planes, while a lot of Tongans joined the army to protect the Pacific. But the single event she is most remembered for around the world, is when she went to Queen Elizabeth's coronation in England. There was a great storm and all the VIP guests had the hoods of their carriages up, but not our Queen Salote. She insisted that the hood stay down, even though it was freezing cold and wet, as a mark of respect to Queen Elizabeth and to acknowledge the thousands of people standing along the road in the rain. So she smiled and waved to all of them. They were so surprised. Many had not seen a brown person before. The English were so impressed they wrote songs about her and she was the highlight along with Queen Elizabeth II being crowned. Everyone wanted to know about Tonga and the brave strong people we must be, to have a Queen like Salote.

Seini, 16 years

Indigenous peoples have the right to set their own priorities and directions for development of their communities. Governments will support indigenous peoples to run their own organizations and services, and in deciding for themselves issues affecting their health, housing and other matters.

(Article 23, UNDRIP)

Artist Mikaela Goulding, 21 years

Tongan Language Lesson

English	Tongan	English	Tongan
Hello	Malo e Lelei	One hundred	Teau
Goodbye	Alu a	One thousand	Tahaafe
Good morning	Malo e tau toe mau'u kihe pongiogini	Man	Tangata
		Married man	Tangata mali
Good evening	Male e tau toe mau'u kihe efi afini	Woman	Fefine
		Married woman	Fefine mali
Yes	Io	Child	Kii leka
No	Ikai	Village	Kolo
Please	Fakamolemole	House	Fale
Excuse me	Tulou Tulou kau kole atu	Market	Maketi
Thank you	Malo Aupito	Shop / Store	Falekoloa
One	Taha	Church	Falelotu
Two	Ua	School	Api ako
Three	Tolu	Eat	Me'akai
Four	Fa	Drink	Inu
Five	Nima	Sleep	Mohe
Six	Ono	Big	Lahi
Seven	Fitu	Small	Si'isi'i
Eight	Valu	Coconut	Niu
Nine	Hiva	Dance	Tau'olunga
Ten	Hongofulu	Play	Va'inga

10 Phrases

What is your name?	Ko hai ho'o hingoa
My name is _____	Ko hoku hingoa ko.......
Where are you from?	Oku ke ha'u mei fei'ia?
I come from _____	Ko 'eku ha'u mei ......
Where are you going?	Ko ho'o alu ki fe'ia
Where is the _____ ?	Ko fee ae....
I would like to go to the beach	'Oku ou fie alu kihe matatahi
What is this?	Ko haa ae mea'a ko eni?
How much does it cost?	Oku fiha ae totongi ae koloa koeni?
What is the time?	Koe ha 'ae taimi?

Indigenous peoples have the right to use traditional medicines and health practices that they find suitable. They have the right to access health care and social services without discrimination. Indigenous individuals have the same right to health as everyone else, and governments will take the necessary steps to realize this right.

(Article 24, UNDRIP)

Tongan Anthem

'E 'Otua Mafimafi,
Ko ho mau 'Eiki koe
Ko Koe ko e falala 'anga
Mo e 'ofa ki Tonga
'Afio hifo 'emau lotu
'Aia 'oku mau fai ni
Mo ke tali ho mau loto
'O malu'i 'a Tupou

English Translation

Oh Almighty God above
Thou art our lord and sure defence
As your people, we trust thee
And our Tonga thou dost love
Hear our prayer for thou unseen
We know that thou hath blessed our land
Grant our earnest supplication
God save Tupou, our king

Children have the right to relax, play and to join in a wide
range of leisure activities.

(Article 31, UNCRC)

Indigenous Peoples have the right to their special and important spiritual relationship with their lands, waters and resources and to pass these rights to future generations.

(Article 25, UNDRIP)

SAMOAN TRIBE

We are all connected.

As some of our ancestors journeyed to Tonga, others sailed to Samoa. Fijians, Tongans and Samoans, at one time, were all one people, sharing similar seafaring skills and a village way of life. Gradually our ancestors established their own 'Tui titles' or kingdoms, the Tui Fiti, the Tui Tonga and the Tui Atua, but our histories remained interwoven. Sometimes there were tribal wars which divided our ancestors. Sometimes there were royal marriages which united them again.

Samoan elders continued to pass down history and traditions. One such legendary folklore is about two maidens who brought the art of tatau (tattooing) from Fiji to Samoa. Another inspiring legend is about Nafanua, a warrior princess who helped establish the cultural traditions of Samoa and is often referred to as a Polynesian goddess who won many battles and brought peace to Savai'i.

Like our other tribes, war and colonisation took its toll on Samoa. Germany, the United States, Britain and later New Zealand, fought over control of Samoa, dividing and redividing until two jurisdictions remained. American Samoa is now a territory of the United States, and Samoa is independent.

Samoans have maintained their Indigenous language and strong cultural traditions. Many people continue to live in fales - grass huts with no walls - and vegetable gardens are maintained. Traditional dancing and tattooing also continue to be performed in the island paradise of two large islands and eight smaller islets. Thankfully today, battles amongst Tongans, Fijians and Samoans are restricted to the rugby field.

Indigenous peoples have the right to own and develop their land and resources. Governments will legally recognize and protect these lands and resources, and will take action to respect Indigenous peoples' laws and traditions in non-indigenous legal systems.

(Article 26, UNDRIP)

Ancient Samoan Legend of Creation

In the beginning, when there was only the heaven, the oceans and the earth. Tagaloa (ancient God) looked down from heaven and decided to create a place on the earth where he could stand. He made a resting place on a rock called Manu'atele or Greater Manu'a. Tagaloa was pleased with his work and decided it would be good to have another resting place, so he divided the Manu'atele further, creating Savai'i, Upolu, Fiji, Tonga and the other islands of the Pacific.

When Tagaloa returned to Samoa, he placed an island halfway between, as a place for the chiefs to rest, called Tutuila. He then ordered a sacred vine to spread over the islands. The leaves of the vine fell and decayed, and then worms appeared. Tagaloa saw that the worms were without heads and legs. So, he gave the worms heads, legs, arms, and a heart, creating man and woman. Tagaloa placed a man and woman on each of the islands that he had created.

Then, *Tagaloa* selected the son of day and night to rule overall. When this boy was to be born, he was given the name *Satia i le Moaatoa* (*meaning* attached at the abdomen), and the whole island group that would be his kingdom was named Samoa (sacred abdomen).

My 2019

2019 was a very crazy year
There was lots of happiness, also a lot of fear
So I will tell you some things that happened
Some joyful moments, and sometimes some tears

In February school has begun
The best place to go, learn and have fun
I met up with my old friends
We talked about our holiday and how it came to an end
Then the school bell rang
And our first 2019 lesson began

Moving along to June
We have Independence Day, starting from morning till noon
My school went for the independence March
Oh, how students wished this day would not last
This day commemorates our country being free
And how we can make it the best it can possibly be

July then came with some heavy rain
Just in time when Samoa was hosting the Pacific Games
Samoa was ready to host the Games when it came along
Then we even made the games its own song
Me and my mates volunteered for the games
We helped out with tennis and met a new friend named James
After all events were over and players have won and earned fame,
All that was left was their Gold medals to claim

Samoan Tribe

October is one of my favourite months
A special day for children to be spoiled by their mums
Having the honour of leading the Church Service with all wearing
white
Treat children as Special Guests from morning till night
Performing and singing for our Special day is a must, to do it right
Expectations from your parents is what you can give without a fight
Monday after White Sunday is a public holiday every year
Making us cool down, before preparing ourselves for final exams
is a fear

November finally arrived
The month for past works to be revived
Exams now nearer than ever
This is the time we really need to be clever
Our teachers now giving us topics we cannot remember
Still we have to try, because the exams starts at the end of
November
The exam day is finally here, lots of hope but mostly fear
Before it starts I do final revision
How long will it take till I get out of this prison

Finally, my exams are done
Now I can go out and enjoy the sun
Straight after that, the measles outbreak began to spread
Causing the whole country to hang by a thread
Schools were cancelled, graduations too
Everyone was mad and sad, but who knew
My dream came near to my graduating year in primary school

Children of the 12 Tribes

Is my final year to be honoured with a sweet send-off on a
Thursday afternoon?
Lots of tears and heartbreak in our classroom when we were
told it's all cancelled
Our safety comes first, who am I to complain, enforcement from
government is final

In December, the measles outbreak became worse
This sickness was so bad, it hit my island like a curse
Stay at home was not so fun
My cousins and I tried to go out for a run
During this time everyone had to be vaccinated
While doctors and scientists tried to figure out where the
disease originated
Doctors and nurses came to help from different parts of the earth
Helping hands from the Pacific, Vancouver, Germany, Hawaii,
and even Perth

My parents decided for my sister and I to go to New Zealand for
a holiday
The feelings of excitement almost drive us insane
A few weeks later we were in the air
When we saw New Zealand, all we could do was stare
We touched down on the runway
I got excited and thought about how long we would stay
From Auckland to Wellington our cousin Kisa is waiting
I could tell every hour that passed she was complaining

Samoan Tribe

When we arrived, we saw our waiting relatives
Then we off to Naenae hills where they live
Christmas was on its way
Shopping non-stop buying clothes, toys and games to play
Then I remembered my family and how the measles had ended
and came to a halt
Too tired to think about it but I'm ready to go back home

Krishna Bawdekar, 13 years

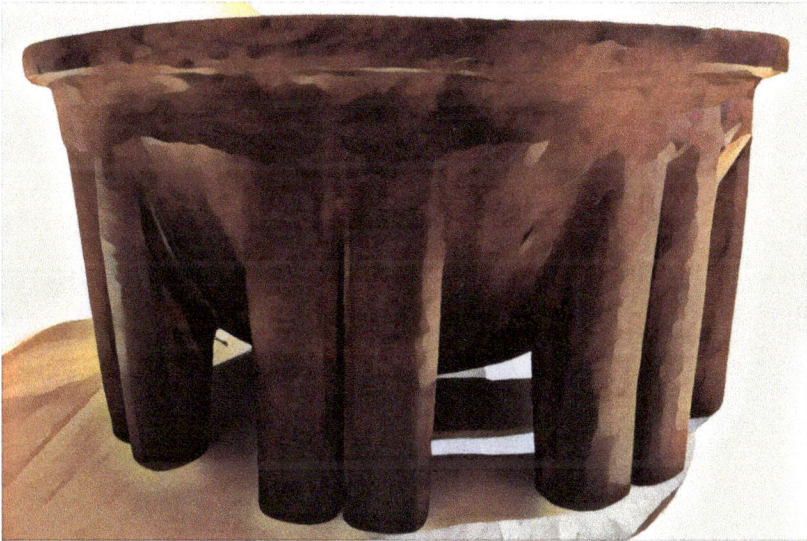

A Samoan New Zealander

In a Samoan family, relationships between family members are very important. As I was growing up in Samoa, my relationship with my grandmother was very tight. When God called her back to Himself, my parents decided it was time for us to move to New Zealand for a better future. Talofa lava o lo'u igoa o Janet Bryce. From birth I was in Samoa, growing up, and this is my story of the obstacles me and my family went through.

Life in the islands was very hard with little opportunity. We lived in Savai'i and my dad worked in Apia, to make sure we went to school and had food on the table. My mother did not work back then, she had to take care of us four children and her parents. I liked how my grandparents lived with us. Even though we didn't have much, family to me was the only thing that matters. Every day was fun because I would play with my cousins and we would all go to the same school. Me and my mother and siblings lived in a small house called a "faleo'o" and my siblings and I attended Gataivai Primary School. We walked to school every morning and had fun along the way. I enjoyed going to school because I loved exploring and learning new things everyday. Living life to the fullest and spending time with family was going well until one day my happiness turned into sorrow.

She died when I was 8 years old, and my world went upside down. It all happened so fast that day. We had white Sunday practice then I was taken quickly to the hospital, then to wait at my aunt's house nearby. It was early morning and I was sleeping when my mum came in, talking with my aunty. As soon as I heard her saying that my grandmother had died, the tears started rolling down my face as I pretended to be asleep. Going back to the village from the hospital was not the same as before, entering her house I felt parts of me were broken into pieces. I wanted to see my grandmother so badly and I was still mourning over her death.

Two years passed, and my parents decided to start a new life where they offer good opportunities and good education for kids. My mum had decided to let my grandfather stay with her sister, and it was time to say our goodbyes to everyone and my old life. That's when we moved to New Zealand. When I first entered New Zealand, it was very cold and very different from Samoa. After the first few weeks of staying in New Zealand, I only enjoyed time spent with my family, but other stuff kept reminding me of home, and how I miss everyone. We stayed at my aunty's house at the time, and I enjoyed how all my dad's family was around because I hardly see them because we lived with my mum's family in Savaii.

Later me and my older sister and little brothers were enrolled in school, and this is where the hard part began. Starting a new school was not easy for me; schools in the islands are way different from schools in NZ. Hearing everyone speaking in English and everything being taught in English was one of the hardest parts of my journey. In Samoa we learnt English, but only the basic words, so I would understand the easy words but when teachers or the kids would communicate with each other, I would just sit there and stare because I didn't understand what they were saying. I looked around the classroom, and it was nothing compared to the classrooms in

Samoa; they have bigger spaces, big desks and everything is clean. Seeing how the teacher teaches the class was very different from what I experienced in the islands.

It was difficult at first, but with the help and support of the teachers I began to understand the school rules and the way of their learning. Also seeing different cultures and meeting new people from different races was not something that I expected to happen. Looking around my class and seeing how there were all different kinds of cultures all around is a gift. It felt as if I'm no longer the odd one out, as we all have a story behind us. I started to enjoy school. Just before the end of the year, my parents had managed to find a new house for us to move in and have our own little family privacy so we can get used to the new lifestyle and start with the challenges ahead of us. It was a three bedroom house, and it was very different from the house I lived in as a child. My mum took a course to help her become a caregiver, and my dad was still hunting for a job for our family to survive but these were happy moments that I enjoyed in NZ, because time spent with family was the only thing that kept me happy throughout all those years.

I started school in intermediate, and we moved again to a different house not far from where we lived before. My parents found new jobs, and us kids were kind of getting used to living the life of New Zealanders. New Zealand was not what I expected it to be. Living in a house does not mean you are living in it for free, I did not know that they had to pay rent, electricity and water. I thought wow, at least in the islands people can build their own house and don't need to pay for it, but in this new life that's not how things work. So luckily for my poor parents to work extra hard day and night, making sure there's food on the table, us kids are happy, and making sure our school bills are getting paid, we managed to get through it. It was hard for them to have so much on their plate and getting used to the new lifestyle here. I wished that I could have done something or be of any help to them, but I am young that I couldn't do anything, so the best thing every parent wants for their children is to make sure they do well in school, because that is the most important thing.

I did well in my previous years in Samoa, but as I got older, I became a disappointment for my parents because school was not going good. I got caught up in trouble and the school would call my mum a few times, and this was very embarrassing and very disappointing. It was times like these that I wished my grandmother was with me, so she would help me improve. I thought of so many things, throughout these past years, about how we grew up in a poor family, and now getting the opportunity to come to New Zealand to start a new life is something other people wished for their family and for that opportunity I am truly grateful.

We moved to our third house, where my aunty and uncle used to live, so they thought it would be great for us to move in, because it is a four bedroom house and much bigger than the last two houses we stayed at. I now realised my parents have been struggling paying rent each month and paying for other things as well, and on top of it all taking care of us five kids was not easy. It's really sad to watch them work hard to make sure there's a roof over our heads. They applied for housing NZ, where they help families that are struggling with rent and other stuff, so they offer houses at low prices, and free water. With the help of Housing NZ, we were told to pack up all our things, and had to stay in a motel for seven days. We stayed at Astro Motel, where we were given two rooms to stay at until they told us to move. It was very small, and the kitchen was shared with other families that were staying there at the motel. Each room had a bathroom in it, and it was very tight for such a big family like mine. Me and my family would pray every day to God to help us in our situation. It was a very different life from what we used to have in the past. I only liked it because it was near my school and I could walk there every morning.

Seven days turned into four months, and by the time we were told to move to a different house to wait until a house under housing NZ is available then we would move there. It was a very long and difficult journey for us, but we did not give up just then. Things were good when we moved away from the motel. It was good to get away from all the bad things we would see and hear while living at the motel. People getting into fights, families having troubles with other families, and sharing a kitchen was one of the worst things ever. I was glad when we moved away, to get away from all these messed up people, and start getting our life back on track. We stayed at the "emergency house" for almost a year, when God decided it was time for us to move again. My parents were so excited when they received the news that a 6-bedroom house is available and if they would be interested in it. My parents were so excited, for their prayers have been answered. I felt very happy that we have received such good news, and it was time again for us to start somewhere fresh outside of South Auckland with a house this big than any of the houses we've lived in before.

Seeing where we are now, with my parents and siblings, I can't stop thanking God for answering our prayers, and for never giving up on us when we were at our worst. My parents don't have to struggle anymore with paying rent, but that doesn't mean they don't have to pay other stuff as well. I am so glad to experience this journey because it will remind me of where I came from and all the obstacles that we've had to face along the way. This experience has taught me so many things in life. I am grateful for many things. It was very hard trying to adapt to the new lifestyle because kids acted differently from the way we were brought up and so it was a challenge. We've overcome many challenges, including housing, adaptation of lifestyle and also the basic culture of New Zealand but as those challenges were passed, we learnt new things and we took those lessons with us every step of the way and with our culture and language always in our hearts we are proud to be here, where we are, living as Samoan New Zealanders. I leave you these words, *"When things go against you, remember that the airplane takes off against the wind."* So, no matter what obstacles you have to go against, remember who you are and where you come from. Fa'afetai tele lava

Janet Bryce
A young Samoan girl, now living in New Zealand

Coronavirus in the Islands

You may not come here with a cough
If you do, I'll see you off
I do not like to see you sneeze
I'll throw you out after one wheeze

You have a fever
You are close to being thrown into a river
You are tested positive with Covid-19
You cannot go near restaurant and canteens

I cannot go to school
But sorry I am not a fool
I will learn at home
And try not to move

It is rare for everything to become still
No sports, no schools, no churches, ohhh this is so unreal
Our usual daily lives are being affected
Just follow orders from government, to make sure everyone is
protected

First time in life, I try this out
Prayers and fasting, yeah, that's what life is all about
Started hard, but it became so sweet
Doing it with my family, when everyone stayed home for a week

Samoan Tribe

Orders for markets and supermarkets to close at four
A stop for boats between islands, wow,
this has never happened before
buses are not allowed to be in service when state
of emergency start
Getting together at least five people, everyone finds it hard

Working hours cut, and layoff from works are normal at this time
That gives a lot of people something new to try
My love for baking grew more while staying at home
A problem to Daddy topping up our cash power almost cost him
a trip to Rome

Until the day a cure is found
Don't bring your germy self around
But wash your hands and get to rest
Will visit you when your health is the best

Maupenei Bawdekar, 11 years

*Children should be protected from any activities that could
harm their development.*
(Article 36, UNCRC)

Samoan Language Lesson

English	Samoan	English	Samoan
Hello	Talofa	One hundred	Tasi Se'lau
Goodbye	Tofa Soifua	One thousand	Tasi A'fe
Good morning	Talofa la'va	Man	Tama
Good evening	Talofa lava	Woman	Teine
Yes	I'oe	Child	Tamai'titi
No	Leai	Village	Nu'u
Please	Fa'amolemole	House	Fale
Excuse me	Mali'e lava lau susuga	Market	Maketi
Thank you	Faafetai lava	Shop / Store	Fale'oloa
One	Tasi	Church	Lo'tu
Two	Lua	School	A'oga
Three	Tolu	Eat	A'i
Four	Fa	Drink	I'nu
Five	Lima	Sleep	Mo'e
Six	O'no	Big	Te'le
Seven	Fi'tu	Small	Lai'titi
Eight	Va'lu	Coconut	Niu
Nine	I'va	Dance	Si'va
Ten	Se'fu'lu	Play	Ta'a'lo

10 Phrases

What is your name?	O a'i lou i'goa?
My name is _____	O lo'u igoa o _____
Where are you from?	O fea e te sa'u mai a'i?
I come from _____	Ou te sau mai _____
Where are you going?	O fea e te a'lu ai?
Where is the _____?	Ou te alu i _____
I would like to go to the beach	Ou te fia a'lu i le Mata'faga
What is this?	O le a le mea lea?
How much does it cost?	E fia le ta'u ?
What is the time?	Ua ta se fia?

*Children who have been neglected or abused should receive
special help to restore their self-respect.*

(Article 39, UNCRC)

Since the beginning, Native Peoples lived a life of being in harmony with all that surrounds us. It is a belief that all humankind are related to each other. Each has a purpose, spirit and sacredness. It is an understanding with the Great Spirit or Creator that we will follow these ways. And in this understanding we believe we are related to all other living species.

Dennis Banks

SENSE OF PURPOSE

Every person is unique and valuable and has a purpose on our planet. Our sense of purpose is a special calling, need or interest that makes our life meaningful. All human beings crave a sense of purpose and may suffer mental health symptoms if we don't have it. Ideally, our purpose is something we love to do, and we are good at it. Having a purpose enhances our self-esteem, helps us to meet our goals and is closely linked to having hope and positive wellbeing.

Indigenous communities are known for having strong collective purpose, promoting their cultures, care for their villages and communities, protecting their traditional lands and their spiritual and religious commitments. It is also important for people to have their own purpose as well. This may include study, a career, art, voluntary service, music or sports.

Keys To A Strong Sense Of Purpose

- It is closely linked to identity, self-esteem and achievement

- It may change and does not need to be a lifelong commitment

- Our tribes provide great opportunities to find purpose and meaning, which in turn can increase our sense of identity and belonging

- We are surrounded by other opportunities; volunteering for a community group, fundraising for struggling farmers, returned soldiers, the homeless or communities impacted by disaster

- When we focus on helping others or the environment, we feel part of something bigger, which improves our sense of wellbeing and happiness.

Through consciousness, our minds have the power to change our planet and ourselves. It is time we heed the wisdom of the ancient Indigenous people and channel our consciousness and spirit to tend the garden and not destroy it.

Bruce H. Lipton

COOK iSLANDER TRIBE

We are all connected.

Our ancestors rested a while in the many islands they had inhabited. Then using their expert seafaring skills once again, some of our ancestors journeyed to Tahiti, before arriving in the Cook Islands, more than 1000 years ago. They settled amongst the 15 islands and enjoyed 500 years living a traditional island life.

Dutch and English explorers arrived 500 years later, followed by missionaries, who discouraged the Cook Islanders ancient religious beliefs and traditions. Kava was forbidden. Sadly, slave traders from Peru, known as blackbirders, came and kidnapped many Cook Islanders, taking them to Peru to become slaves.

Like other Pasifika people, Cook Islanders live in villages and are renowned for their traditional crafts including woven pandanus baskets, mats and fans. Cook Islanders are also expert traditional dancers and drummers. Many continue to speak their Indigenous languages, including Cook Island Maori. Cook Islanders practice tivaevae, a combination of appliqué and embroidery. Tivaevae decorated bedspreads and cushion covers are highly regarded in the Pacific.

In 1995, France resumed nuclear-weapons testing in the Pacific. A Cook Island crew of traditional warriors was sent in a vaka (traditional voyaging canoe) to bravely protest near the nuclear test site.

Today, many Cook Islanders live and work in New Zealand and support family members at home in the Cook Islands.

My Island Story

Hi, my name is Timothy Jnr Anitonia and I'm 10 years old. My dad's name is Timothy Anitonia as well, so you can call me TJ for short. I'm a proud multicultural boy. I'm multicultural because my dad's a Cook Islander and my mum's Fijian and they met in Australia. First, they had my brother Elijah in 2005, my sister Havanna in 2006 and they saved the best for last, me in 2009.

I always feel safe at home because I have caring and loving family members and I'm glad God gave me the blessing to have this family. To me, this family is precious as I am safe and secure in a family where I am loved and supported. My family is always there when I need them, even if I have been naughty.

My family are not just my parents and my siblings, my family includes uncles, aunties, grandmas, grandpas, cousins, nephews, nieces and even family friends that are not related. This is my Cook Islander and Fijian family.

Being a Cook Islander makes me feel safe because it makes me feel more confident about myself and being Fijian at the same time makes me feel safe because I have many talents that I can feel proud of. I love this because I can feel good about myself and know where I came from and where I belong.

My mum always tells me I am Australian because I'm born here but to never forget that I am also a Cook Islander and Fijian.

Timothy Jnr Anitonia, 10 years

This Is The Place I Was Born

I am Elijah, and I am of mixed blood,
Cook Island and Fijian, can't deny this stud!
I'm also Australian, believe it or not,
Let's go back in history, see what I've got,

I was born in Australia, on the 4th of June,
I grew up loving sports and playing video games in my room,
I started to play guitar, strumming and making noise,
But when I played for God, that's when I would enjoy,

I am from the church of New Life AOG,
I praise and worship, with the music ministry,
People love everything they have heard,
But the one thing that touches them is our Pastor's preaching
the word

My parents train the young leaders in a troop
Our young leaders are called the youth group,
We are also the Music Ministry, in the flesh,
We are a kindful group, young and fresh

This is the place where I belong,
This is the place where I stand strong,
Australia is the place to be,
Australia, the place that I love, you and me.

Elijah Anitonia, 15 years

Artist Havanna Antonia, 14 years

Cook Island National Anthem

Te Atua mou ē

Ko koe rāi te pū

O te pā 'enua ē

'Akarongo mai

I tō mātou nei reo

Tē kāpiki atu nei

Pāruru mai

I a mātou nei

'Omai te korona mou

Kia ngāteitei

Kia vai rāi te aro'a

O te pā 'enua ē

English Translation

God of truth

You are the ruler

of our country

Please listen

to our voices

as we call to You

protect and guide us

and give us Your crown of truth

so we can be successful

and so that love and peace will rule forever

over our beloved country

Cook Islands Language Lesson

English	Cook Islands Maori	English	Cook Island Maori
Hello	Kia Orana	One hundred	Tai anere
Goodbye	Ka kite, Aere ra, Noo ake ra	One thousand	Tai tauatini
Good morning	Kia Orana	Man	Tane
Good evening	Kia Orana	Woman	Vaine
Yes	Ae	Child	T#Tama
No	Kare	Village	Oire
Please	Ine	House	Are
Excuse me	I na ake ra	Market	Makete
Thank you	Meitaki maata	Shop / Store	Are toa, are okooko
One	Tai	Church	Pure
Two	Rua	School	Apii
Three	Toru	Eat	Kaikai
Four	A	Drink	Inu
Five	Rima	Sleep	Moe
Six	Ono	Big	Maata
Seven	Itu	Small	Meangiti
Eight	Varu	Coconut	Akari
Nine	Iva	Dance	Ura
Ten	Tai'ngauru	Play	Kanga

10 Phrases

What is your name?	Ko'ai toou ingoa?
My name is _____	Ko _____ toku ingoa.
Where are you from?	No'ea mai koe?
I come from _____	No _____ mai au.
Where are you going?	Te aere nei koe ki ea?
Where is the _____ ?	Tei'ea te _____ ?
I would like to go to the beach	Ka inangaro au I te aere ki te pae taatai
What is this?	E'ea teia?
How much does it cost?	E'ia moni I te oko?
What is the time?	E'aa te ora?

Governments will respect and recognize Indigenous peoples' laws and traditions about land and resources and take action to have these respected in non-Indigenous legal systems. Indigenous peoples have the right to get help from governments to protect their lands.

(Article 27, UNDRIP)

Indigenous peoples have the right to get back or to be compensated when their lands, territories or resources have been wrongly taken away, occupied, used or damaged without their free, prior and informed consent.

(Article 28, UNDRIP)

NiUeAN TRiBe

We are all connected.

As some of our ancestors journeyed to the Cook Islands, others sailed to Niue, a giant coral atoll, 260 square kilometres in size. These ancestors settled there and continued to enjoy their traditional village lifestyle, with plenty of seafood available. Captain James Cook, the English explorer who claimed much of the Pacific for Britain, attempted to land in Niue. Perhaps these ancestors had heard from their Pasifika brothers and sisters that things had not gone well after visits from Captain Cook, because Niuean warriors repeatedly challenged him and scared him and his crew away. He named Niue, Savage Island and other Europeans stayed away for many years afterwards.

Missionaries eventually landed and Niue was colonised by the British and then handed to New Zealand. Niue is now an independent state. War, cyclones and tsunamis have taken their toll on Niue.

Many people have moved overseas for employment and further education, and there are less than 2000 people living in Niue. Despite this, they continue to practice their traditions and culture, including the haircutting ceremony for teenage boys and the ear-piercing ceremony for baby girls.

Like other Pasifika people, Niuean are expert subsistence farmers and grow taro, cassava and kumara, and have developed noni fruit and vanilla for exporting.

Niuean Tribe

An Australian Umu

Keep the newspapers
We are having an umu
Keep catalogues too

Cut the onions
Then wash and cut the polo
Make sure there's enough

I brought some brisket
Are there enough newspapers?
I'll bring some more rocks

Tea? Coffee? Milo?
Mum! Mum! Do you want coffee?
Argh! There's no more milk!

I made takihi
Can it fit in the umu?
And I have chicken

We went to the shop
Was this the one you wanted?
That's all that was there!

Co'Erina Kamupala, 20 years

Indigenous peoples have the right to their environment being protected. Governments will respect and protect the right of Indigenous peoples to develop and protect their lands, water bodies and other natural resources.

(Article 29, UNDRIP)

Niuean Language Lesson

English	Niuean	English	Niuean
Hello	Fakaalofa lahi atu	One hundred	Taha e teau
Goodbye	Koe kia (1 person) Mua kia (2 people) Mutolu kia (3+ people)	One thousand	Taha e afe
Good morning	Fakalofa pogipogi atu	Man	Taane
Good evening	Mafola nakai afiafi	Woman	Fifine
Yes	E	Child	Tama
No	Nakai	Village	Maaga
Please	Fakamolemole	House	Fale
Excuse me	Tulou(when walking in front of elders) Fakamolemole mai la (to get attention)	Market	Makete
Thank you	Fakaue	Shop / Store	Falekoloa
One	Taha	Church	Faletapu, Faituga
Two	Ua	School	Aoga
Three	Tolu	Eat	Kai
Four	Fa	Drink	Inu
Five	Lima	Sleep	Mohe
Six	Ono	Big	Lahi
Seven	Fitu	Small	Tote
Eight	Valu	Coconut	Niu
Nine	Hiva	Dance	Koli
Ten	Hogofulu	Play	Pele

10 Phrases

What is your name?	Ko hai e higoa haau?
My name is _____	Koe higoa haaku ko _____
Where are you from?	Hau a koe he kavi fe?
I come from _____	Hau au i _____
Where is the _____ ?	Ko fe e _____?
Where are you going?	Fano ki fe a koe?
I would like to go to the beach	Fia fano au kehe mataafaga
What is this?	Koe higoa ae?
How much does it cost?	Fiha e tau?
What is the time?	Kua ta e hola fiha?

Indigenous peoples have the right to decide how they wish to develop their lands and resources. Governments must respect and protect these rights. Indigenous peoples' free, prior and informed consent must be obtained when any decisions are made that may affect the rights to their lands, resources or waters.

(Article 32, UNDRIP)

Niuean National Anthem - Ko e Iki he Lagi

Ko e Iki he lagi
Kua faka'alofa mai
Ki Niue nei
Ki Niue nei
Kua pule totonu
'E he patuiki to 'atu
Kua pule oko'oko
Ki Niue nei
Kua pule oko'oko
Ki Niue nei
Kua pule ki Niue nei

English Translation - Lord of Heaven

Lord of Heaven
You show mercy
To Niue
To Niue
You rule righteously
You, the Great King
You rule supremely
Over Niue
You rule supremely
Over Niue
You rule over Niue

We must pay close attention to those with another imagination: an imagination outside of capitalism, as well as communism. We will soon have to admit that those people, like the millions of Indigenous people fighting to prevent the takeover of their lands and the destruction of their environment - the people who still know the secrets of sustainable living - are not relics of the past, but the guides to our future.

Arundhati Roy

Sense of Wellbeing

Wellbeing is not just about physical health. It is also how you feel about yourself and your life. Wellbeing means happiness, resilience and life satisfaction. The main factors influencing wellbeing are :

1. A partner or good friends
2. Enough money for security
3. Regular exercise for 30 minutes four to five days a week
4. A diet with lots of lean proteins (meat or fish) and fresh fruits and vegetables
5. Enough sleep
6. Spiritual or religious beliefs
7. Fun hobbies or activities
8. A healthy self-esteem and an optimistic outlook
9. A sense of purpose
10. A sense of belonging

Indigenous people used to have a very healthy lifestyle, with all of the top 10 factors needed for wellbeing. Following colonisation and the introduction of Western diets and lifestyles, Pasifika people are now amongst the unhealthiest in the world with high rates of diabetes, heart disease and obesity. Returning to a traditional diet full of fresh meat, fruits and vegetables without processed salt and sugar can help improve the health and wellbeing of Indigenous people.

Indigenous people are famous for having good friendships and social interactions, whether they live in villages, towns or cities. They know their neighbours, bus drivers, school and work families – everyone. Social activities are frequent. Church and community duties are still a main part of life there. Schools and villages work together to raise funds for basic items.

The true indicator of wellbeing and resilience is not how you feel when everything is great, but how you cope in times of crisis and even grief. When someone dies, traditional rituals and ceremonies can bring stability, and the built-in social and family networks provide support. People will cross the country or the ocean to contribute money, food, mats, tapa cloth, yaqona and willing hands to cook, clean and care; not just for a couple of hours, but for days and weeks. After the funeral, celebrations of the person's life continue, allowing healing, sharing of happy memories and helping loved ones to move on with life.

The Heart Foundation provides practical advice to make staying physically healthy simple. Eat wholesome, nutritious foods, do regular physical activity, monitor your blood pressure and cholesterol, be smoke-free and try to stay optimistic and enjoy each day. They also provide lots of advice, resources and recipes, and it's free to all on their website, www. heartfoundation.org.au.

Remember to maintain strong relationships with family and friends and make time for regular face-to-face catch-ups and real contact, not just on social media. If people are at risk, there are places to get help and that includes your family doctor, as well as family and friend networks, counselling - which is often available through employment assistance programs - or mental health plans through doctors. Many countries have Lifeline 24/7 phone support for children and adults.

Keys To A Strong Sense Of Wellbeing

1. Wellbeing is not just about diet or exercise, there are resources available (such as the Heart Foundation) to assist you to improve your wellbeing

2. Positive relationships and social interactions are the strongest predictors of a long life

3. Financial security can be important to wellbeing, ask for help to develop a simple budget and financial plan

4. Indigenous people often have a strong sense of purpose which is also important for wellbeing

5. Resilience in crisis is well developed in many Indigenous communities due to stability created by ceremonies and rituals. Everyone has a role to play and they know how to be present and how to provide and accept support.

Indigenous peoples have the right to decide what their identity or membership is. They also have the right to decide who their members are according to their own customs and traditions. Indigenous peoples have a right to be citizens of the country in which they live.

(Article 33, UNDRIP)

TOKELAUAN TRIBE

We are all connected.

As some of our ancestors journeyed to Niue and the Cook Islands, others were landing on the atolls of Tokelau. After they settled, like their other Pasifika brothers and sisters, they established chiefly clans, occasionally took part in tribal battles and relied on fish and coconut to survive.

When the Europeans came, they brought Christianity, and the Tokelauan community embraced the new religion. This led to some significant changes in Tokelauan society. Trading ships brought also brought new types of foods and materials. Unfortunately, like the Cook Islands, in the 1860s, Peruvian slave ships kidnapped nearly all of the men so they could use them as slaves in Peru. Many of the men died from disease and few survived or were able to return to Tokelau. With most of the men gone, Tokelauans set up the Taupulega, the Councils of Elders.

Tokelau became part of the British Empire in 1877 and was then passed to New Zealand in 1926. Tokelau remains part of New Zealand but have maintained their distinctive culture and language. Tokelau is just five metres above sea level, and despite being coral atolls, they cultivate crops such as breadfruit, taro, bananas, papaya, pumpkin and coconut.

Our Tokelauan brothers and sisters are working hard to protect their greatest asset; natural marine resources which provide the majority of their national income.

Tokelau is a climate change world leader and hopes to be the first nation in the world to achieve 100% renewable energy.

Tokelauan Tribe

What Makes Me Happy?

My Name is Scarlett Mele Metcalfe. I have a twin sister, and together we dance and learn about our Pacific Island culture with the group Ala Mai. My Dad is from Tokelau and my Mum is from New Zealand. I was born in New Zealand and I am very proud of where I come from; it is very important to my family. When I grow up, I want to be an Astrologist who learns about the planets and universe.

Play all day
Friends become family
Ala Mai makes me happy

Learning to dance
Finding out new things
Ala Mai makes me happy

Singing makes me calm
Swaying to the drum
Ala Mai makes me happy

I feel protected
Cared for and safe
Ala Mai makes me happy

Scarlett Metcalfe, 7 years old

A Tokelau Letter

Hi Everyone,

My name is Paige and I am 7 years old, about to turn 8.

I am from lots of places - isn't that amazing. I am half Tokelauan and I am a New Zealander. When I grow up, I would like to be a Pacific Island dance teacher because I am very good at dancing. I would like to follow my dreams and do it for my culture to show I care.

Our dance group, Ala Mai is on YouTube and we do a lot of performances. I love doing all the dances and learning new songs. I am so happy I belong there; I am in love with it. My group is called Ala Mai. Ala Mai is the best. I just love being a part of it and making new friends. I feel safe at Ala Mai because I have amazing tutors who help us all so much.

One day I want to go back to my dad's island, Tokelau, so I can see where I come from and learn dances from that place. We want to take my nana with us, from New Zealand because she hasn't been home for a long time. She will probably cry. I can't wait to swim in the sea and watch dad catch fish and meet lots of new cousins. I love having lots of cousins!

I miss my cousins in New Zealand, so mum takes us to Ala Mai, so we make new cousins. They all feel so special to me.

Paige Malena Metcalfe, 7 years old

Tokelauan Language Lesson

English	Tokelau	English	Tokelau
Hello	Malo ni	One hundred 101	Helau
Helau ma le tahi	Tofa ni	One thousand	Afe
Good morning	Manuia te taeao	Man	Taulelea Tamaloa
Good evening	Afiafi	Woman / Girl	Fafine / Teine
Yes	Io	Child / Children	Tama / Tamaiti
No	Heai	Village	Nuku
Please ·	Fakamolemole	House	Fale
Excuse me	Tulou ni	Market	Maketi
Thank you	Fakafetai	Shop / Store	Falekoloa
One	Tahi	Mass / Church	Lotu / Falesa
Two	Lua	School	Aogo
Three	Tolu	Eat / Food	Kai / Meakai
Four	Fa	Drink	Inu
Five	Lima	Sleep	Moe
Six	Ono	Big	Fuaefa
Seven	Fitu	Small	Taigole
Eight	Valu	Coconut	Popo
Nine	Iva	Dance	Hiva
Ten	Hefulu	Play	Tafao

10 Phrases

What is your name?	Ko ai to igoa?
My name is _____	Toku igoa ko.....
Where are you from?	Koe e haku mai fea?
I come from _____	Ko au e hau mai......
Where are you going?	Koe e fano ki fea?
Where is the _____ ?	Tefea te.......?
I would like to go to the beach	Ko au e fia fano ki te matafaga
What is this?	Hea tenei?
How much does it cost?	E fia te tau?
What is the time?	Kua ta te fia?

Indigenous peoples have the right to their own structures, traditions and laws in ways that ensure that Indigenous peoples enjoy the highest standards of human rights.

(Article 34, UNDRIP)

Tokelau's National Anthem - Viki o Tokelau

Te Atua o Tokelau

Te Atua o nuku, te Atua o Tokelau

Fakamanuia mai ia Tokelau

Puipui tauhi mai ko ito filemu

Toku fenua, tau aganuku

Tau fuka ke agiagia

Lototahi, tumau hi to fakavae

Tokelau mo te atua

Te Atua o Tokelau

Hoa, he hoa lava

English Translation

The God of Tokelau

The God of villages, the God of Tokelau

Do bless Tokelau

Carefully tend the peaceful ito

My land, your custom

Your flag that's waving

Of one mind, stand firm as a foundation

Tokelau for God

God of Tokelau

Indigenous peoples have the right to decide what responsibilities individuals in their community have towards the community as a whole.

(Article 35, UNDRIP)

New Pasifika Tribe

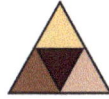

We are all connected.

All human beings belong to one species called Homo sapiens. There is only one race of people on Earth, called the human race. We are all descendants of the same African tribe. Colonisation has given us many labels for Aboriginal and Pasifika people based on physical traits and European perceptions; Melanesian, Polynesian, Micronesian, Australoid, Austronesian, Lapita descendants, the list is endless. Perhaps it is better for us to look at what we share, what all have in common amongst our 12 tribes and beyond.

We share rich ancient history, living bright culture, strong spiritual and religious beliefs, and deep connection to land, family and our tribes. Just as our ancestors changed and adapted to their new environments, so have we. As our tribes have settled, mixed and migrated, we now look different from some of our ancestors. We may be darker or fairer, our hair may be straighter or curlier, even blonde. Instead of tribal battles, there are sports like rugby and football. Many Pasifika people are gifted singers, musicians and dancers. We have also moved into business and now we are accountants, pilots, chefs, nurses, doctors, lawyers and teachers. It's important to remember that no matter where we now live on Earth, all humans have remained genetically 99% the same and we carry our ancestors' stories as well as their physical traits in our DNA.

Some of us struggle with our identity when we aren't just one colour or one culture. Disconnection or rejection from our tribes can be devastating because we are all driven by the need to belong; to our family, our tribe and our place. By learning to embrace our tribes, we can develop our superpower, cultural fluidity; the ability to bridge the gap and walk between different worlds.

As Indigenous peoples, we know there is more to the world. We know spirits exist. We know as women, because we're especially attuned to this kind of knowledge, that spirits exist and have a presence in our lives. Some of us are gifted and can communicate with the spirit world. Not everyone has that gift and can perceive the borders between the living and the dead and our society actively discourages us of exploring the knowledge of what many of us have already always known in our cultures.

Sandra Cisneros

DNA Anomaly

My name is Keanu, I am 13, almost 14 years old, and I am a DNA Anomaly because I have more than one set of DNA - I've got Fijian, Tongan, Irish, Chinese, African, Russian and probably another thousand that I lost track of. My parents have all kinds of different cultural ancestors - it's insane.

I was born in Melbourne, Victoria but moved to Fiji when I was six weeks old and spent the first few years of my life being raised in the islands. Cool right? After the army took over in 2006, my family moved back to Melbourne, where my younger brother was born. We still try and visit Fiji every year to see family, go fishing and sail on the Whale's Tale, which is the best.

I have a place that makes me feel like I belong and unfortunately, it's every child's nightmare, school! I know right, the terror, the teachers, the homework, but school's not all bad. You've got friends there that are very loyal (I hope) and the reason I feel like I belong in the community is because of my friends and school being the location that makes me feel welcome.

I have hobbies - I like music, sport, movies and video games (but mostly music and sport). I like the drums and I like tennis - these are my favourite things to do in my free time when I don't have time-wasting homework! Seriously.

I have my own security as the book states, self-security. I've got karate, so I don't have to worry about fights or any type of violence which could result in me being hurt or others - not that the time will come, but it is always good to come prepared and expect the unexpected. I have a big Pacific family I belong to, which is cool.

Life is pretty good in Australia, but when we go to Fiji, it's pretty good there too.

Keanu Robert Goulding, 13 Years

Indigenous peoples living in different countries have the right to be in contact and carry out activities with each other. Governments, in consultation with Indigenous peoples, will support Indigenous peoples in exercising this right.
(Article 36, UNDRIP)

Fade to Black

Raged
Accusations
Covered
In
Sadistic anger
Manifested

Byron, 17 years

Governments will respect all the agreements they have made with Indigenous peoples. The Declaration in no way reduces the rights of Indigenous peoples in other agreements previously made by Indigenous peoples with governments.

(Article 37, UNDRIP)

Governments and the United Nations, including the United Nations Permanent Forum on Indigenous Issues, should work with Indigenous peoples to make sure the rights of all Indigenous peoples as provided by the Declaration are realized and protected.

(Part 8, UNDRIP)

CULTURAL SUPER POWERS

The ability to walk between two worlds, such as Indigenous traditional communities and modern western society, is referred to as cultural fluidity. It is the understanding of the differences between two cultures, appreciation for the history, the language, rules and rituals and the ability to live and interact positively in either world.

Business and world leaders are finally developing their own levels of cultural fluidity; learning about other languages and cultures to improve relationships with other countries and promote peace during conflict and grow business opportunities in an increasingly globalised world.

Cultural fluidity is a talent and a skill - a superpower that has become increasingly valuable. In business diversity and appreciation of Indigenous language and culture is a sustainable competitive advantage. Learning from cultures which have thrived for thousands of years in a sustainable way is good for business, as well as the community.

Putting All The Pieces Together – DNA Action Plan

There is a DNA vision board, checklist and action plan at the end of the book, to assist you to develop your cultural super powers, using the information below.

Sense of Security

Food, water, shelter and freedom from fear are human needs. A stable home and enough money are also important to develop a sense of security. Racism and discrimination is still a global issue and is usually triggered by fear and ignorance. Having a response plan ready for school, the workplace and when out in a community can help ease the negative impact of racist bullying.

Remember:
1. Your safety and security always come first!
2. Have a racism response plan ready, with actions such as:
   - ignore it
   - if it is safe, tell the person their behaviour is offensive and not okay
   - report incidents to a teacher, manager, the police or your Human Rights Commission.
3. Oceania people are great entrepreneurs who can turn their talents into creative and successful businesses.
4. A simple budget and financial plan can help ease financial stress and anxiety for everyone with:

- 50% – Security expenses including mortgage/rent, food and bills
- 10% – Tithing, extended family, church or community commitment
- 10% – Pay off loans and credit cards and don't use these anymore
- 10% – Savings for long term home or business
- 10% – Savings for children/education

5. Solidarity amongst a family, community, our tribes and our countries allows our voices to be heard locally and around the world.

Sense Of Belonging

Being accepted for who you are is the most important aspect of belonging, first by your family, next by your tribe and then community. Regular check-ins with family are really important, not just in times of crisis, but also to remind people they have support. Strong friendships and social groups at school, work or in the community also help people feel like they belong.

Oceania people who move overseas and away from their traditional connections may struggle and lose contact with elders, their traditional place and culture. It is never too late to reconnect. If you can't connect with family or visit your traditional land remember you can form your own tribe of friends, or a community group with a positive common interest to strengthen your sense of belonging.

Learn all you can about the language and the culture. Information is readily available online. Better yet, record your family history from elders or link in with people who have the same background and culture as you do. Armed with knowledge and basic language, you can visit your traditional land and tribe and enjoy genuine connection with people who have the same ancestors as you.

Sense Of Identity

1. It's important to identify positive role models from your tribes and spend time learning language, history and culture
2. A DNA test can assist you in identifying your ethnic background, but results aren't always what you expect
3. Self-esteem and identity are closely linked
4. Acknowledge the good and the bad history, and move forward
5. Be proud of who you are and where you come from.

Sense Of Purpose

A sense of purpose is also a human need and is vital for our wellbeing and happiness. Failing to have one may contribute to poor mental and physical health. Our purpose doesn't need to be a lifelong commitment and it can change over time. Finding a way to help someone else is a great place to start.

Setting short and long term goals can help strengthen your sense of purpose - how about writing a story, a poem or a song, or creating artwork for a book?

Sense Of Wellbeing

The most important factor in developing a sense of wellbeing is maintaining positive relationships. These are more important than diet and exercise. Together, security, belonging, identity, purpose and wellbeing make up the DNA five senses and building blocks of our cultural triangle.

Sometimes pieces of a person's cultural triangle are stolen or damaged, but it can heal and be strengthened with the support of family, tribe, traditional and western healers and the community.

Remember - We are all one people and we are all connected.

DNA Action Plan Checklist

Security

- o I have a home
- o I have enough food, clean water and warmth
- o I know that racism and discrimination is illegal, and I have a response plan
- o I have a simple financial plan with a budget to achieve my short and long term goals

Belonging

- o I maintain regular contact with my trusted family members
- o I maintain friendships or ask for help from trusted family, teachers and elders
- o I share an interest or am a member of a sports or community group
- o I choose to learn about my Indigenous language, history and culture
- o I have visited my traditional country and have connected with my village or clan

Identity

- o I have positive cultural role models I can connect with
- o I have positive role models or mentors in the country I live in

- o I choose to learn about my Indigenous culture
- o I can confidently identify my nationality and background
- o I understand my history and I choose to learn from it and move forward

Purpose

- o I focus on helping others at home, school or in the community
- o I choose my purpose which may be religion, sport, health, music or art
- o I choose to pursue study or a job which will strengthen my sense of purpose
- o I understand that purpose may change over time and that is okay
- o I understand that a strong sense of purpose is key to my wellbeing

Wellbeing

- o I choose to be grateful for five things every day
- o I have at least one positive family relationship and friendship I rely on for support
- o I choose a healthy diet with traditional foods, and do fun exercise five days a week
- o I get a minimum of 7-8 hours of sleep each night
- o I appreciate my traditional connections to land, tribe and culture

DNA MANA - Vision Board

A vision board is a collection of words and images which represent your wishes or goals. Some goals may be long term and years away. Others may be short term and achievable within weeks or months. Your vision board can inspire and motivate you to achieve your goals.

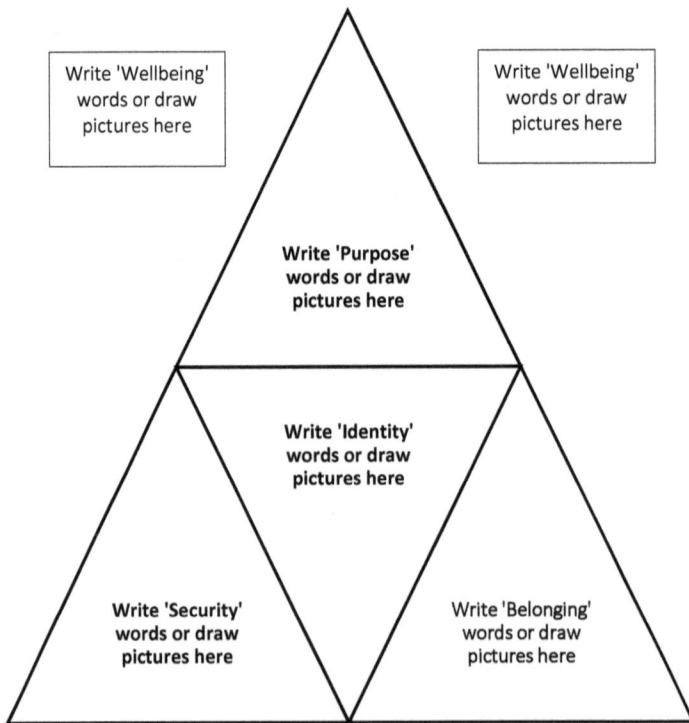

Write 'Wellbeing' words or draw pictures here

Write 'Wellbeing' words or draw pictures here

Write 'Purpose' words or draw pictures here

Write 'Identity' words or draw pictures here

Write 'Security' words or draw pictures here

Write 'Belonging' words or draw pictures here

Put your vision board up in a special place where you can see it daily. If you don't have your own space, create your vision board in a diary or planner.

Check out www.diversitynetwork.com.au for DNA Mana – Vision Board resources.

My DNA Plan

Name _____

SMART Goals are - Specific, Measurable, Achievable, Realistic, with a Timeframe. Create an annual DNA plan using the this template.

Review your goals every month to make sure you are on track. Sometimes, goals may change. A plan and your commitment means you are making progress.

Goals	Action Steps	Time	☐
Security			
Belonging			
Identity			
Purpose			
Wellbeing			

Check out www.diversitynetwork.com.au for DNA Plan resources.

My DNA Finance Plan And Budget

Finance Goals (example: pay off loan or school fees, buy sewing machine)
1.
2.
3.

Budget – Income And Expenses	
Income (Monthly)	$
Take home pay	$
Rental/land royalties income	$
Government payment	$
Other	$
Total Income $	
Expenses (Monthly)	$
Tithing / soli /community contribution (10%)	$
Mortgage or rent	$
Loan repayment	$
Credit card repayment	$
Children (clothing, childcare, school fees etc)	$
Groceries	$
Insurances (house, car, health, life etc)	$
Electricity	$
Water	$
Phone / Mobile	$
Gas	$
Internet	$
Personal (clothing, toiletries, medical)	$
Entertainment / Going out / Takeaway	$
Transport (car, bus, boat fares etc)	$
Other	$
Total Income $	

Total Income-Total Expenses = Savings For My Finance Goals

Check out www.diversitynetwork.com.au for finance plan and budget resources.

REFERENCES

Colour Outside The Lines: One Girl, Two Tribes, 2019, Bernie Goulding

www.abc.net.au/news/science/2016-10-04/dna-reveals-lapita-ancestors-of-pacific-islanders-came-from-asia

www.shareourpride.org.au

www.education.vic.gov.au/about/programs/bullystoppers

Tackling Racism in Australia, A Unit of Work for the Australian Curriculum Health and Physical Education, Australian Human Rights Commission

www.hrc.co.nz/news/give-nothing-racism

What Makes Us Happy, Professor Robert Cummins, Deakin University

Racism. It Stops With Me, Community Service Announcements, 2017, Australian Human Rights Commission

Scanlon Foundation Mapping Social Cohesion Surveys 2016, Professor A Markus

www.betterhealth.vic.gov.au

www.thekingdomoftonga.com

www.timorleste.tl/east-timor

www.gov.nu/wb/pages/the-island.php

www.tokelau.org.nz

www.un.org/development/desa/indigenouspeoples/declaration-on-the-rights-of-indigenous-peoples.html

www.unicef.org/child-rights-convention

1. Connect with us –

Subscribe to DNA for free updates and exciting new products from our communities : www.diversitynetwork.com.au

2. Free Bonus Gifts for a limited time only

Download your free DNA Vision Board, Action Plan and Training eBook here at: www.diversitynetwork.com.au

3. 50% discount for the first 100 customers

Children Of the 12 Tribes, on Amazon, Kindle Edition and -

Colour Outside The Lines, One Girl, Two Tribes, on Amazon Kindle Edition : www.diversitynetwork.com.au

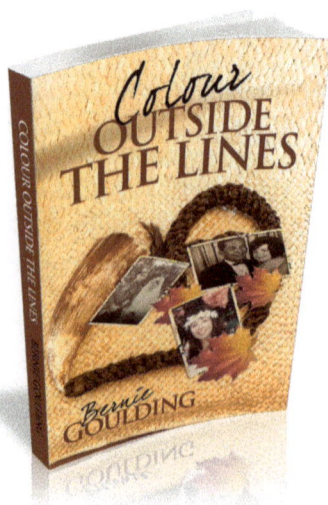

ABOUT THE AUTHOR

Bernie Goulding was born in the Victorian town of Hamilton and is one of seven children. She is a descendant of WWI and WWII ANZACs, hardworking farmers, teachers and nurses. She is also a descendant of Fijian warriors and cannibals, German aristocracy and Chinese merchants, with an extended family around the world too numerous to count.

An Australian-trained nurse, Bernie volunteered as a public health sister at Korolevu in Fiji and lived in a grass hut (bure) working with local medical teams to improve indigenous health, often using traditional remedies. With the Fiji Red Cross, Bernie developed a specialised war injuries workshop for United Nations Peacekeepers serving in Lebanon, Sinai, Iraq and Cambodia. She introduced training for prisoners as part of a community rehabilitation program and coordinated emergency standby teams at sporting and school events, civil disturbances and following natural disasters like cyclones and floods.

To combat high drowning tolls in the Pacific, Bernie partnered with the Commonwealth Royal Lifesaving Society and a team of local volunteers, training thousands of children to Swim and Survive. Together with the University of the South Pacific, her lifesaving programs were extended to students from 13 other Pacific island nations.

Bernie has been a speaker at national conferences in Australia, the UK and Fiji. She developed the OHS blueprint for the Fiji Sugar Corporation, the Ports Authority of Fiji, Sheraton Resorts Fiji and the Ownership Model for CUB Ltd and the WorkSafe Victoria Award-winning Scope SAFE Program for Scope Australia. She is also a member of the Pacific Women's Indigenous Network.

Bernie proudly identifies herself as a Fijian Australian and has gained over 30 years nursing, training and management experience in health community services, occupational health and safety, lifesaving and human resources in Australia and Fiji. She now lives in Melbourne with her husband John and their three children, Mikaela, Keanu and Malakai. Bernie now leads a health and safety team in the disability sector and remains committed to supporting Indigenous communities in the Oceania Region.

ACKNOWLEDGEMENTS

I wish to acknowledge the traditional owners, the Wurundjeri People as the original custodians of the land and I respect their customs and traditions and their special relationship with the land on which I grew up and now live. I would also like to acknowledge the traditional owners of Naroi and Vunuku in Moala, Lau, Fiji, the island of my ancestors, to which I am bound.

In 2018, I wrote a book called, 'Colour Outside The Lines: One Girl, Two Tribes.' It wasn't perfect, but it was my story about growing up part Fijian, part Australian with some Irish, Chinese, Tongan, Samoan, German, English and maybe even some Timorese thrown in. My daughter Mikaela completed all the illustrations and the photos. To date, 'Colour Outside The Lines: One Girl, Two Tribes,' has travelled to 25 countries in Oceania, the Middle East, Africa, Europe and North America.

The idea for this book was sparked at the Human Rights and Peoples' Diplomacy Training Program in Timor-Leste in August 2019. I was honoured to be amongst 30 community representatives from across Asia Pacific, given the opportunity to strengthen our knowledge and skills in international human rights standards and mechanisms. For 12 days we had United Nations global experts as our teachers, we celebrated Timor-Leste's 20th anniversary of the vote for independence and we shared the aspirations of human rights defenders from 19 countries in our region.

I made many special Pasifika friendships in Timor-Leste, with young people from Papua New Guinea, West Papua, Fiji and Timor-Leste. Is Timor-Leste part of the Pacific you may ask? Their ancient history, language, food, culture and way of life, their connection to land and sea, not to mention their strong Christian beliefs are so similar, I have no doubt they are. The Timorese have a great deal to share with us and witnessing their wisdom, resilience, unwavering faith and ability to forgive was certainly the most humbling experience of my life.

So, the seed was sown in Dili and Balibo in Timor-Leste, then grew through social media amongst the 12 tribes, who answered our call. We asked young Pasifika people of all abilities to share their stories - what makes them feel safe, like they belong, what strengthens their senses of identity and purpose and finally what makes them happy.

Vinaka vaka levu and obrigada to the Diplomacy Training Program, Isidor Kaupun, Cipri Neves, Ruland Levy, Gasper Afonso, the Anitonia

Acknowledgements

family, the Metcalfe family and Tokelau Melbourne Mataliki Sport and Culture, Louise Byrne, Bernadette Rounds Ganilau, May Goulding, the Rumbiak family, Anne Pakoa, Emma Kamupala, the Baleisuva family, and all of the *Children of the 12 Tribes* who participated. Fakaue also to the Pacific Women's Indigenous Network and to the Victorian Fijian, Cook Island, West Papua and Niue Associations for their support and assistance with language translations as well. Much love and gratitude to Mikaela Goulding for her amazing art work in linking all of our tribes over our 65,000 year journey.

Finally, vinaka, malo and thanks to all of you, the people of my tribe.

Loloma and with much love,

Bernie Goulding

DNA's Oceania Planners!

DNA is excited to be launching planners in 2021, created by and for young Pacific people. Our planners contain great advice and tips to improve security, belonging, identity, purpose and wellbeing in challenging times. There are fantastic plan, budget and vision board templates, as well as unique Indigenous art and fun language facts too. Stay tuned!

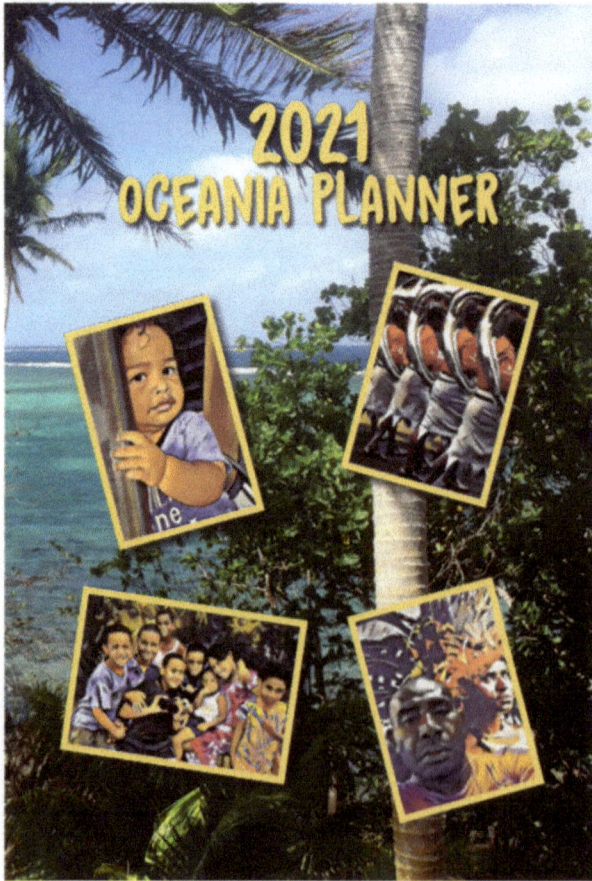

NOTES

www.ingramcontent.com/pod-product-compliance
Lightning Source LLC
Chambersburg PA
CBHW052113030426
42335CB00025B/2961